Niki de Saint Phalle
A–Z

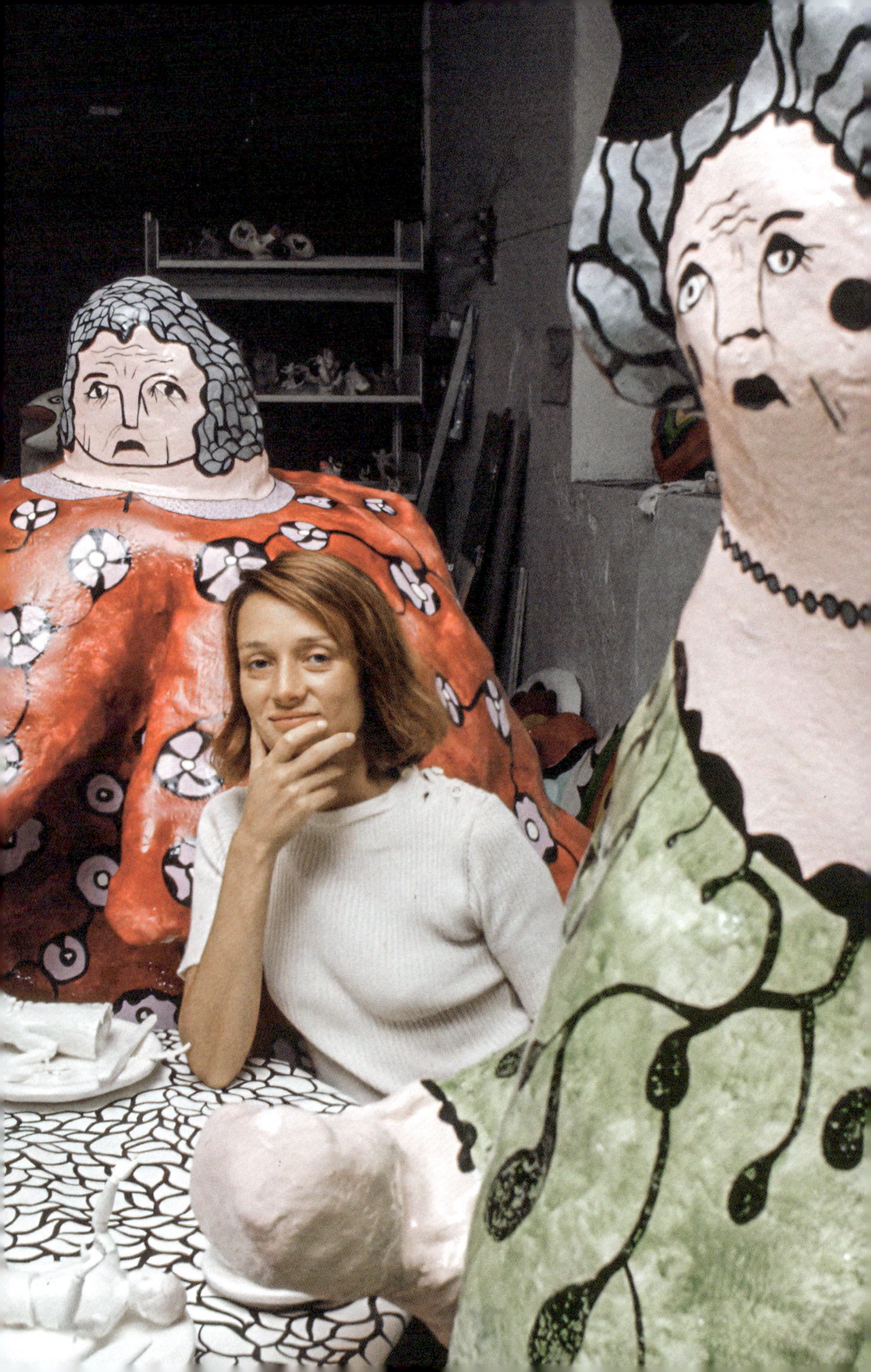

Niki de Saint Phalle
A–Z

Katharina Sykora

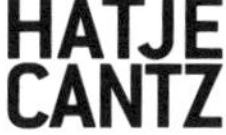

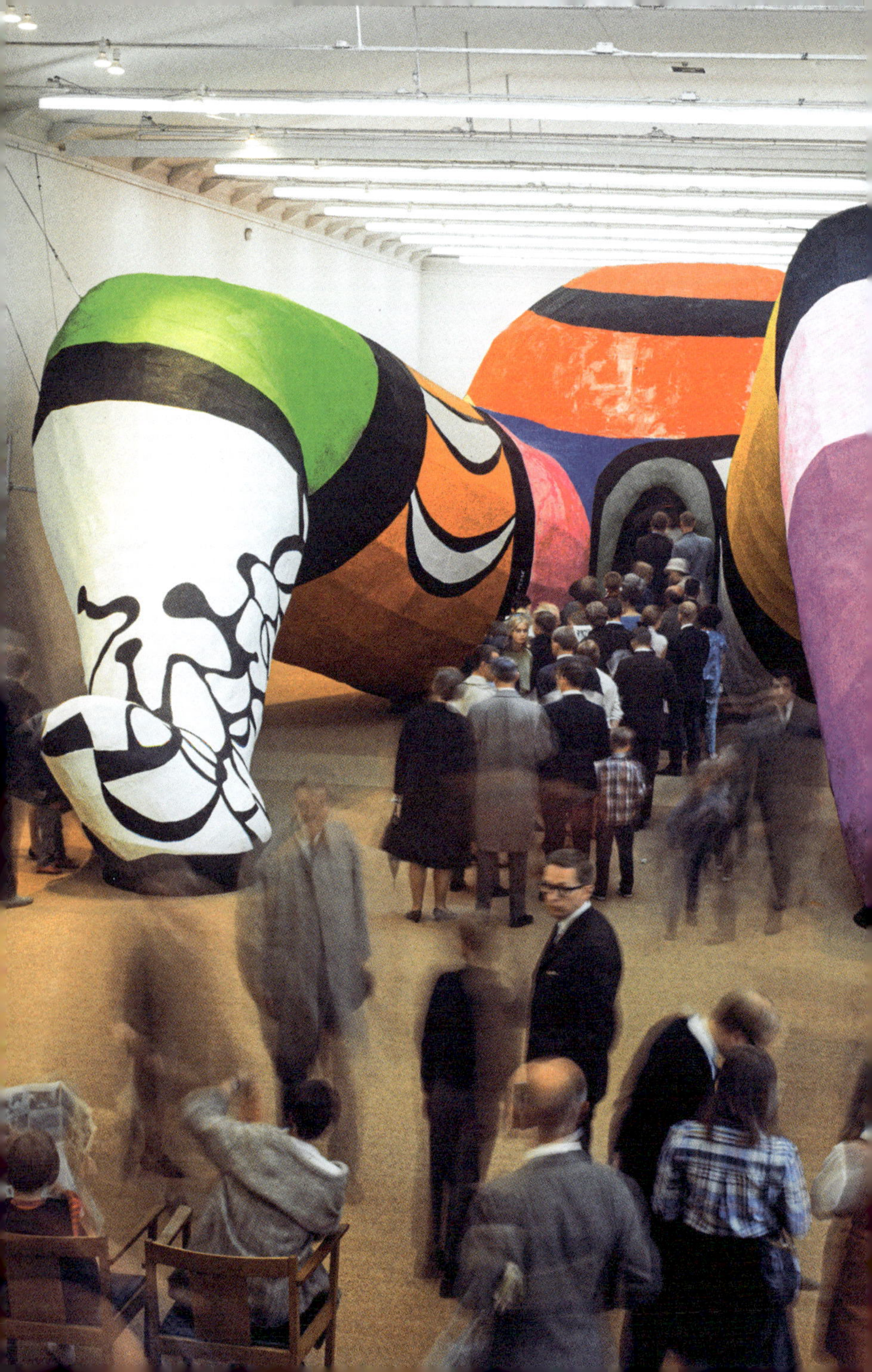

A→ AIDS

The year is 1986. The illness already has an official name: AIDS, which stands for acquired immunodeficiency syndrome. When the illness first began to appear in the early 1980s, it represented a great unknown for doctors and was usually fatal to those who became ill. That triggered fears worldwide and led to those affected being ignored.

Niki de Saint Phalle had many friends who suffered that fate. As a politically aware person who did not separate the personal from the social and viewed the body as a physical, spiritual, and social authority, she became an AIDS activist.

Niki de Saint Phalle herself suffered from an immunodeficiency and therefore knew experts in the field. She turned to the specialist Dr. Silvio Barandun from Bern and with him collected facts and advice for an educational book. To keep these commandments and prohibitions from seeming like the Tablets of the Law, Saint Phalle expressed them as a fictive letter to her son, Philip. He belonged to the generation that had grown up in the era after the prudishness of the postwar, a time of sexual liberation thanks to modern contraceptives, and was thus at risk of getting AIDS.

In another rhetorical maneuver, she emphasized not warnings but rather the permitted, emancipatory aspect of a sex life with information about AIDS. That is already reflected in the title: *AIDS: You Can't Catch It Holding Hands*. →pp. 7–9 Moreover, her verbal and visual humor →Laughter mitigated the harsh tone of the cautionary directives, and she supplemented them with amusing examples of cases and colorful illustrations. For example, the toilet seat that cannot infect us becomes a bull's-eye with a view of the broad sea, and the first-person narrator cheerfully offers condoms decorated with colorful snakes and hearts for safe sex and declares with a wink that nuns, monks, and faithful couples are the winners in the Russian roulette of AIDS.

Niki de Saint Phalle had begun this work 1982 and was thus ahead of her time. The book was published four years later in the United States and Germany, in 1987 in France, and then in Italy and Japan. She worked with

USE A RUBBER

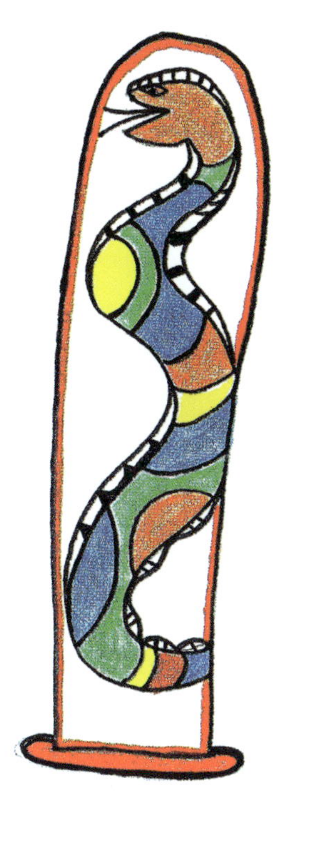

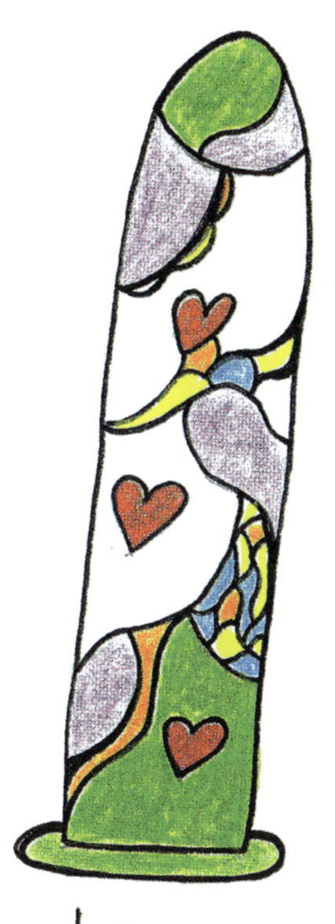

← what do you think of these?

It may not be your cup of tea but it will save lives.

AIDS: You Can't Catch It Holding Hands (detail) 1986

YOU CAN'T CATCH it FROM

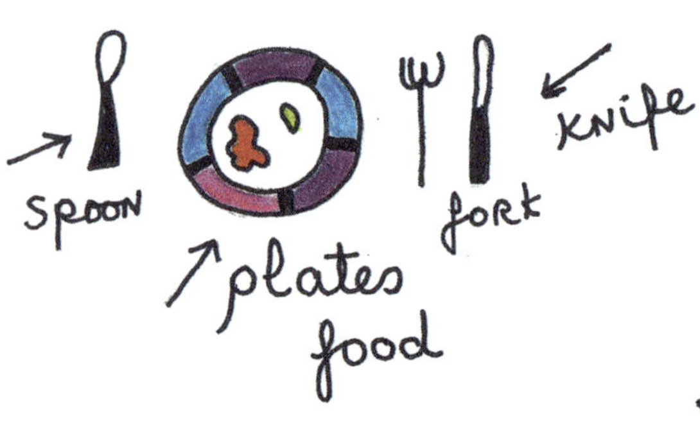

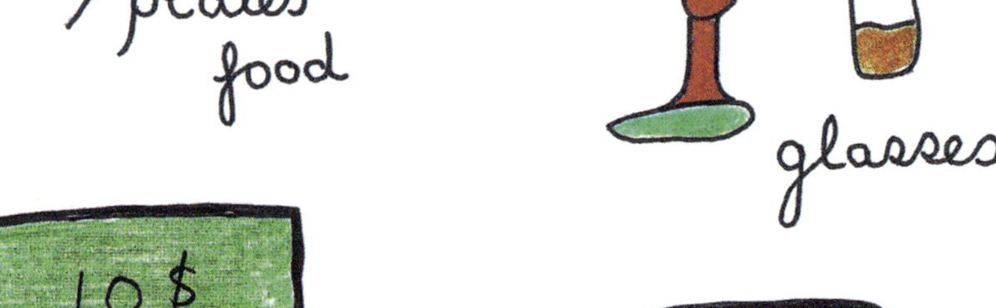

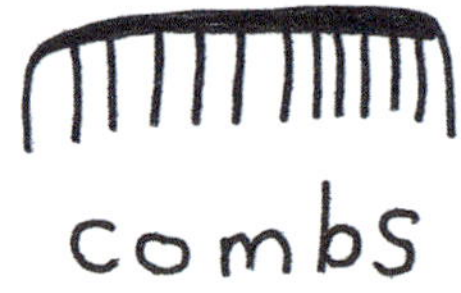

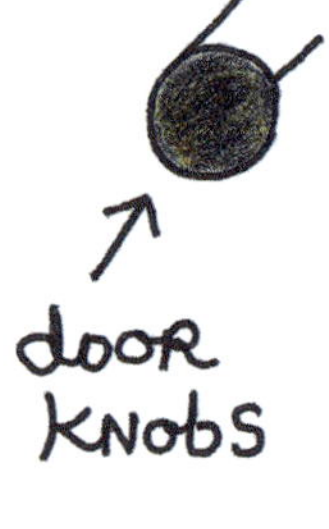

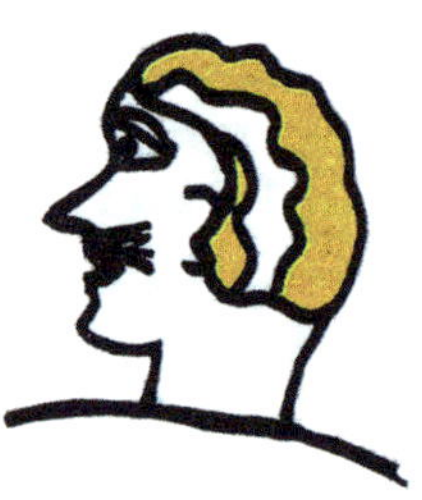

AIDS: You Can't Catch It Holding Hands (detail) 1986

TEENAGERS

BE CAREFUL AT PARTIES
with drink and drugs.
(or you may forget your resolution)

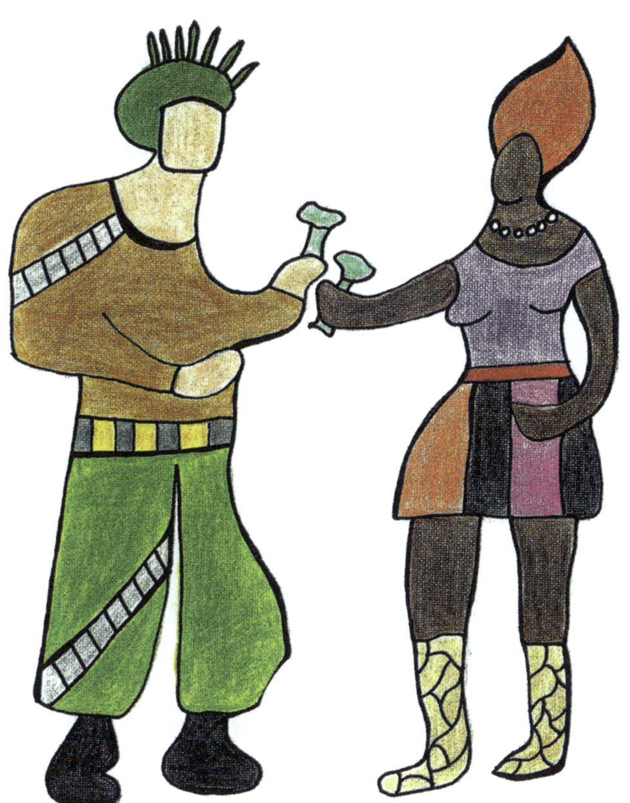

AIDS: You Can't Catch It Holding Hands (detail) 1986

initiatives in those countries, provided information for organizations, and had thousands of copies distributed for free in France.

The strength of the book lies in clearly articulating her own fears and those of others, presenting alternatives, and regaining through (self-)irony the self-confidence that makes it possible to be active again in the spirit of ACT UP.[1] Her double educational strategy had two directions: *against* the spread of the virus and *for* gender and sexual diversity.

B → Bride

Niki de Saint Phalle began her artistic career in the early 1950s in the medium of painting and in the 1960s became internationally famous for her spectacular shooting events.→Shooting Between 1963 and 1965, she once again expanded her artistic spectrum and turned to designing three-dimensional figures. She created female figures from papier-mâché on a wire-mesh frame. Then she decorated the figures with textiles and objects and painted over them. These figurative assemblages were not yet freestanding like the later *Nanas*,→Nana but instead relief-like, as if they were to be pressed into the flatness of a painting. And indeed, Saint Phalle would lean several figures against the exhibition walls, mount them on boards, and sometimes surround them with a frame. By connecting back to the place and medium of painting in this way, she was reflecting on the close intertwining of conventional images of femininity and the traditional genre of painting. Saint Phalle's female figures thus transgress all the more obviously established concepts of beauty and role models.

This happens most strikingly in the *Bride* reliefs and sculptures. In Western cultures, the ideal of the bride is on the threshold between child and woman and traditionally associated with innocence, virginity, and purity. Wedding fashion reflects this archetype. The bride wears white and the cut of a wedding dress often follows the hourglass silhouette of the sweetheart line with its emphasis on breasts, narrow waist, and posterior.

Niki de Saint Phalle exaggerated these forms that signal the paradox of hypersexuality and virginity and literally drove to the surface the contradictory phantasms hidden behind the ideal. She covered her *Brides* entirely in white paint, which makes them look as if all life has been removed from them and they seem like embalmed mummies. She had these figures make the gestures of the *Venus pudica*, with one hand chastely in front of their breast and the other covering their pudenda. But she turned this gesture into its opposite: her *Bride* demonstratively points one oversized hand toward the place where the sex is buried in an outsized lace skirt; or the bride's fingers point to a yawning crater on her upper body in place of breasts or heart.

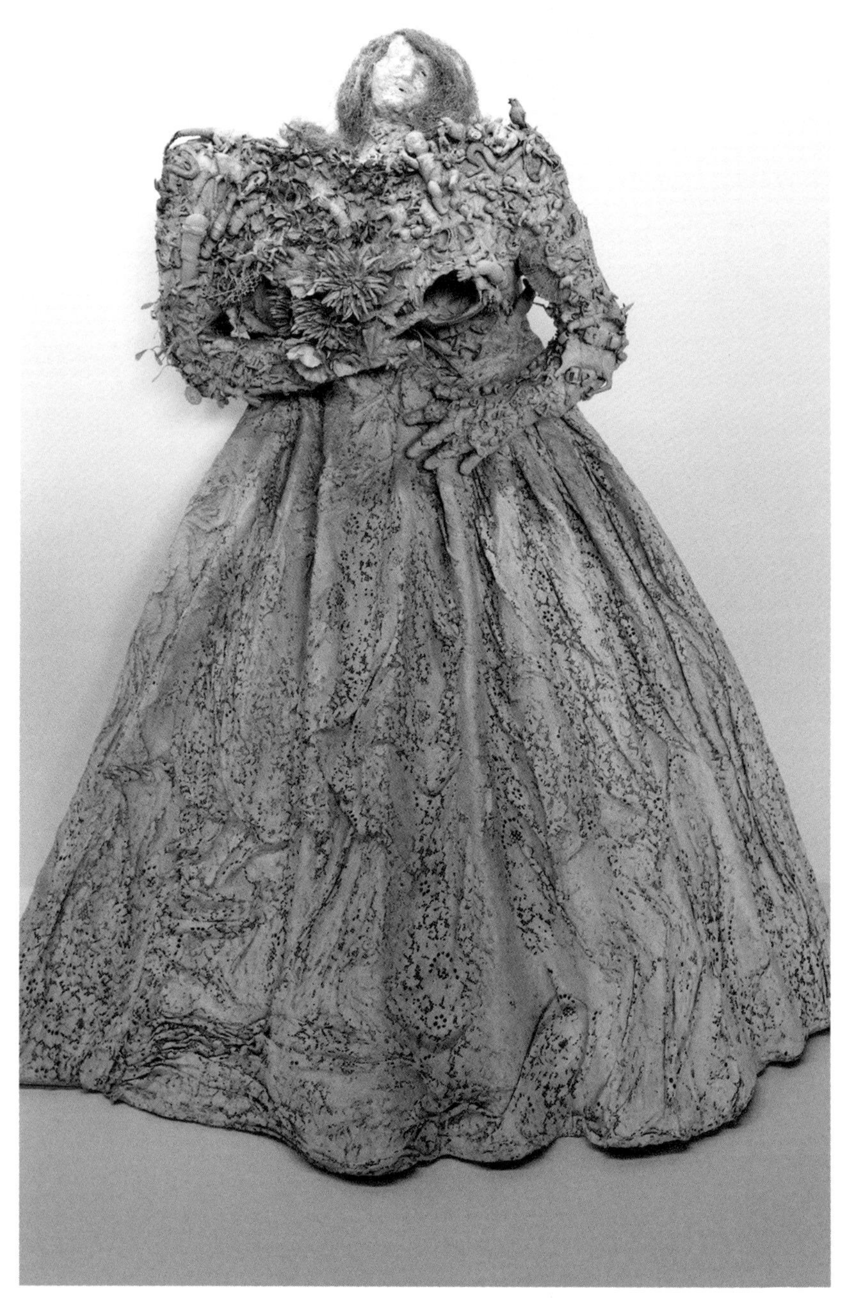

La mariée (*The Bride*) 1963 226 × 200 × 100 cm

Concealing and revealing become ambiguous actions in Saint Phalle's *Brides*. The appliqués she applies to the upper bodies of the figures also follow this logic. Flowers, plastic animals, and numerous baby dolls combine to form a mesentery that transforms the *Bride*'s intact body into an erupted, sprawling surface. Niki de Saint Phalle transforms in the *Bride*'s body the contradictory expectations of femininity as being simultaneously radiating animalistic, a delicate flower, and a mother bearing numerous children into a collision of heterogeneous objects. Like the medieval German Christian vanitas →Vanitas figure "Frau Welt" (Lady World),[2] she is at once attractive and repulsive, teeming with life and permeated by death. The artist was not, however, interested in affirming Christian morality. On the contrary, she was displaying its destructive power with which it both symbolically and literally burdens women.

C→ Chroma

Colorfulness is the first association with Niki de Saint Phalle's works. The artist went through several phases of working with the qualities of the tone and saturation of color, and especially with the consistency of the application of paint and the ground. Initially, she experimented with nuanced contrasts of bright colors with white, gray, or black. Only with her large-scale sculptures did she transition to a chromatic process that completely covered her works with bright colors.

In the early assemblages sealed entirely with white paint, like the *Brides*,→Bride Niki de Saint Phalle still employed the traditional symbolism of white as a sign of purity. In the *Shooting Paintings*,→Shooting she hid the color behind the monochrome surface of the painting and then brought it out through the "shooting wounds" as a spectacular, dynamic flow of color. The beige tones or noncolors of the assemblages became the skin through which the color "bled out" on its own as a result of its artist's premeditated injury. Red often played a central role: it linked the symbolic process of bleeding to the human and, specifically, female body. But the *Shooting Paintings* cannot be reduced to the allegory of the wounded pictorial body since Saint Phalle increasingly drew multicolored fluids from her assemblages. Their flowing, semitransparent consistency and matte ground does not, however, allow these colors to shine. They do not radiate cheerfulness.

Not until the *Nanas*,→Nana with their positive associations, were colorfulness as a strategy and polyester paint employed. It was the era of Pop Art, the Flower Power movement, and enthusiasm for plastic. In the mid-1960s, Niki de Saint Phalle slowly began to remove her three-dimensional female figures from their palette of beige and pink and to cover them with colorful decorations and pictograms. Their secondary sex characteristics were often given ornamental accents of their own that integrated on an equal level into the overall structure of colorful patterns and emblems.→Emblem In this way, they were quite casually revealed from the sphere of hidden shame and became part of the symbolism of the polymorphous pleasure of the senses.→Polymorphy

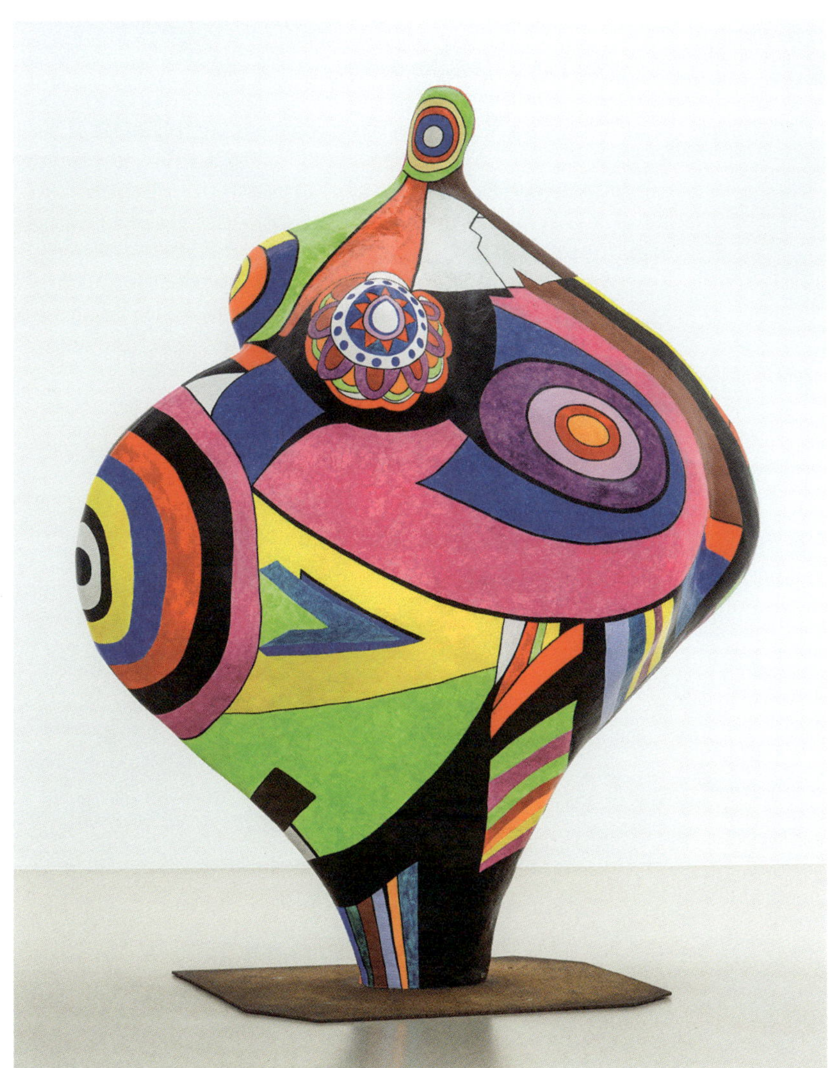

Gwendolyn 1966–90 coated polyester, paint, on wire mesh 252 × 200 × 125 cm

The smooth, glossy polyester paint, whose saturation heightened the effect of the diverse colors, amalgamated the physical forms of the sculptures and the decoration into a single colorful surface. This produced a paradoxical effect in the relationship of figure and ground: the chroma flattened the plastic form, and the plastic form curved the color into the three-dimensional. Like a colorful tattoo over the entire body, it is no longer possible to distinguish between color and background, image and support.

The artist cleverly took advantage of that to smuggle political commentaries about skin color and its coding into her colorful figurations. Her large *Nanas* and *Nana* balloons have every conceivable skin color, from bright blue by way of yellow to red. Niki de Saint Phalle's chromaticism eluded the color scheme of racism and heralded the utopia of social diversity without boundaries. → Xenophilia

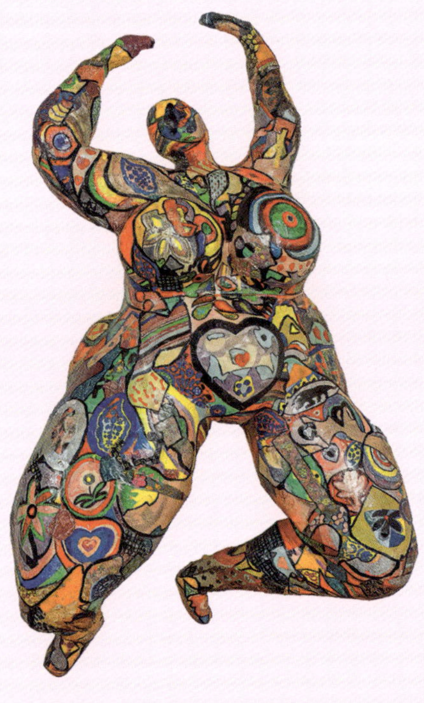

Lili Ou Tony (Lili or Tony) 1965 painted polyester resin, fabrics, wire mesh, and paper 206 × 130 × 130 cm

D→ Dragon

In many cultures, the dragon is the ur-image of overpowering violence that threatens human existence. It is the center of many myths and fairy tales. The dragon entered Niki de Saint Phalle's imagination early on and took on different meanings in her personal emblems.→Emblem

It appears as a synonym for male sexuality and represents the power to destroy the integrity of women. In her drawing *The Monster Dies* (1968),→pp. 18/19 the dragon becomes the symbol of individual experience. It is the animal embodiment of the abusive father,→Film whom the artist symbolically kills to regain control. In *Dear Laura* (1980), the letter writer, alias Saint Phalle, invokes her friend not to permit the dragon of domestic work and childcare to eat her up. The monster has become a synonym for Chronos, the ancient god of time, to whom everything must be subordinated, even Eros. Here, the dragon is an emblem of society's exploitation of women through domestic work and childcare. It stands for the structural principle of the patriarchy.

In an impish recourse to Christian iconography, Saint Phalle transformed this theme from the battle of the sexes into a story of domestication. In a New Year's card to Pontus Hultén →Hon in 1981, she referred to Paolo Uccello's painting of Saint George (1470).→p. 20 According to the legend, he injured the dragon who was holding a king's daughter prisoner with his lance so that she could take the monster into the city on a leash. This miracle of taming the dragon led to many conversions including that of the princess. In his painting, Uccello employs a medieval practice of depicting several episodes in a single image. Saint Phalle subtly varies the temporality of the scene in that the female figure already has the dragon on a leash before her savior can rush up from the distance with his sword drawn. The monster and the armed man appear as two facets of a figuration of male power and violence, though the woman counters them quite calmly. She has chained up the dragon twice, turns her back on her belated "savior" and goes her way.

In Niki de Saint Phalle's tarot symbols,→Tarot the dragon takes on another meaning in its domesticized form. Tarot Card XI presents it as a symbol of the power of the

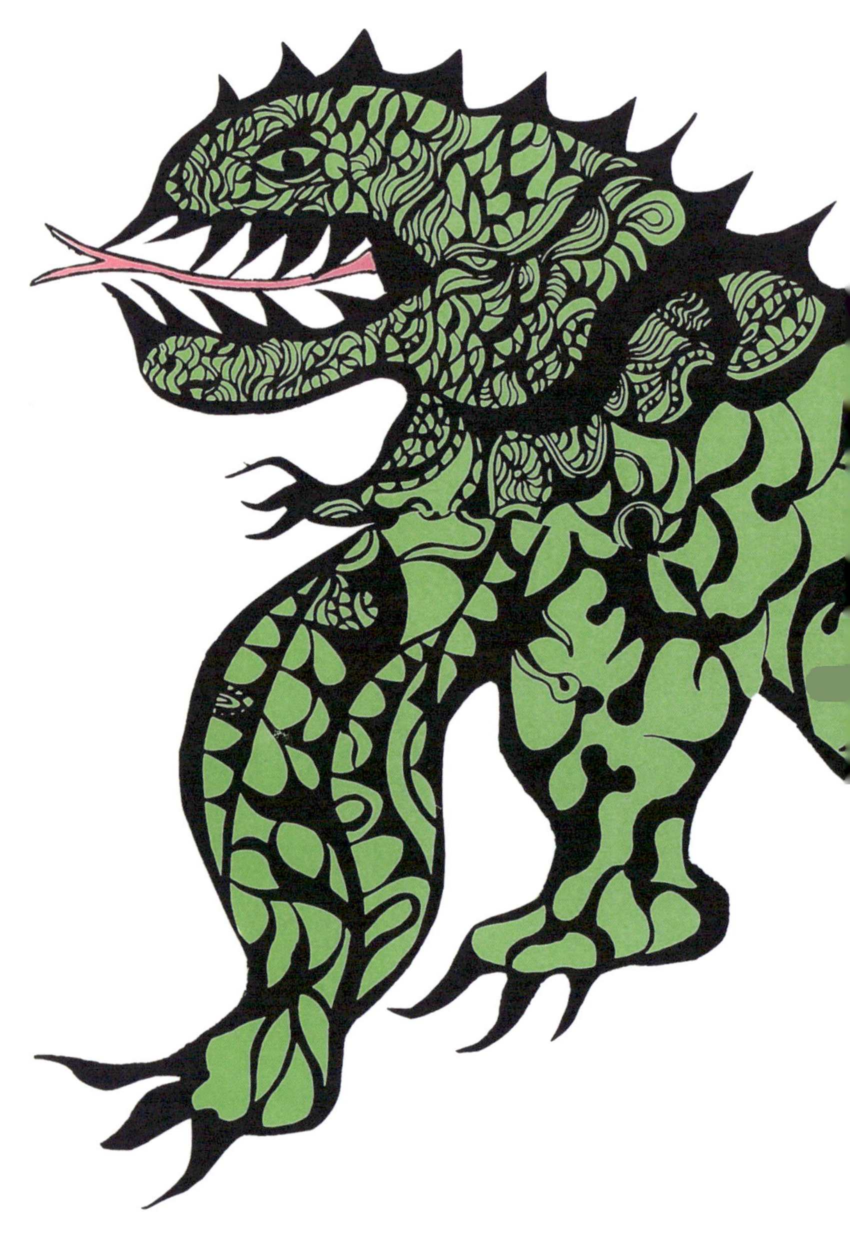

The Monster Dies/I Am the Beautiful White Bird 1968 screenprint 60.1 × 107.6 cm

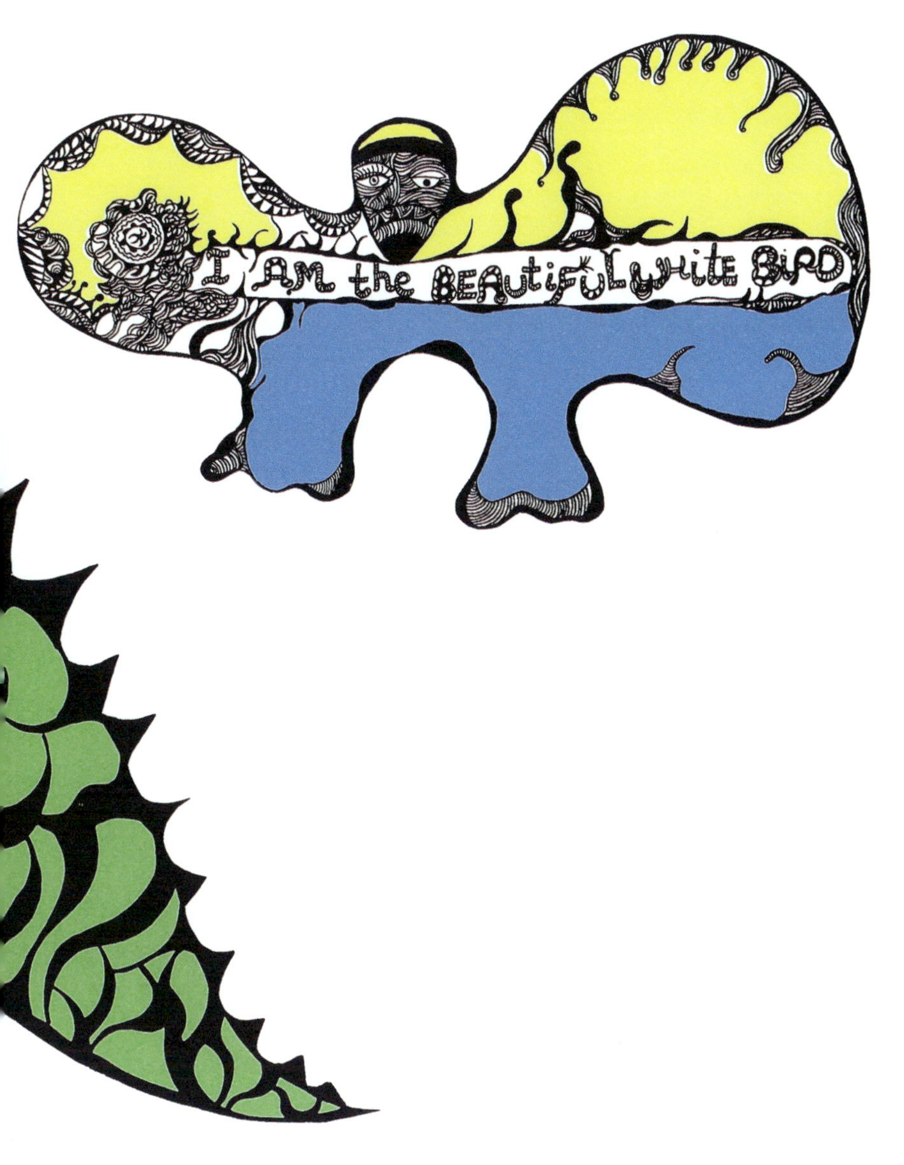
I AM the BEAUTIFUL WHITE BIRD

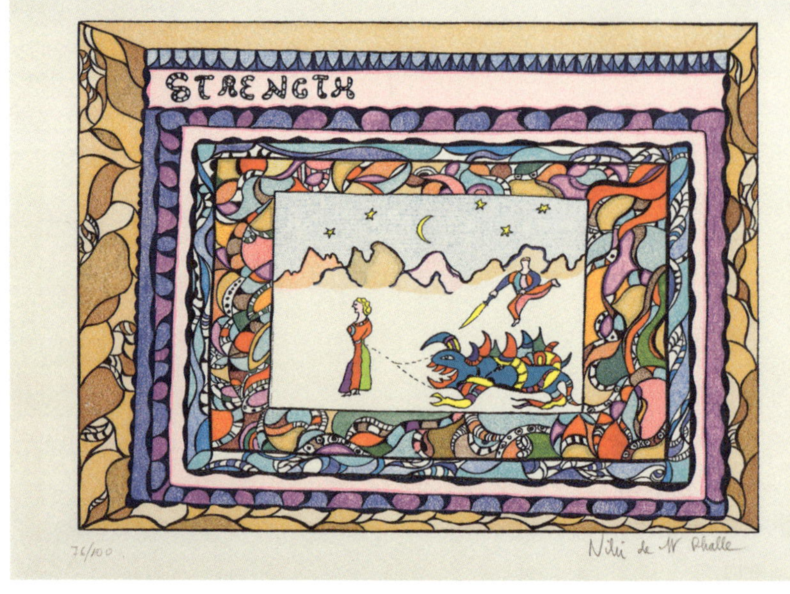

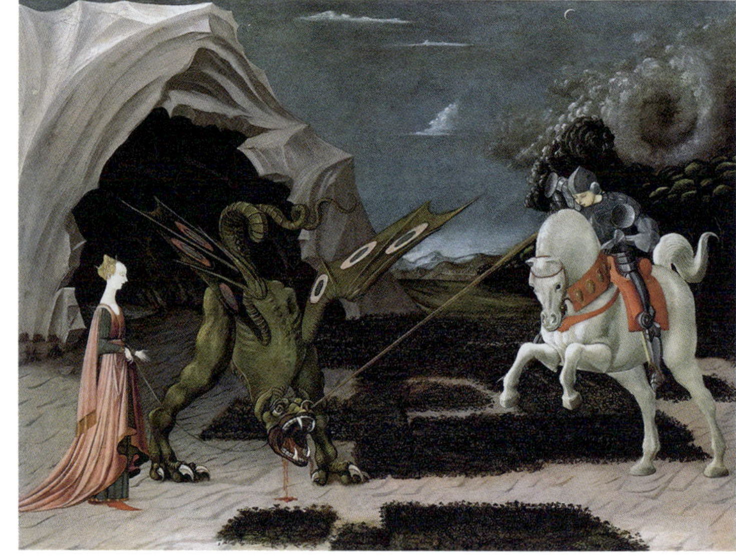

Strength 1973 woodcut 38.5 × 52 cm
Paolo Uccello *St. George and the Dragon* ca. 1470 oil on canvas 57 × 73 cm

woman who defeats it: "Strength/card No. XI/Caph/Love is stronger than lions and dragons/Only Love conquers all," it reads.[3] And in her ode to Jean Tinguely,→Jean Tinguely "You Are My Love Forever and Ever and Ever" (1968), her love is given the attribute of the dragon and lovingly and ironically called "my Tyrannosaurus Rex."[4] In her film *Un rêve plus long que la nuit* (*A Dream Longer than the Night*, 1976),→Film the dragon is the tame guard of the little princess's throne. And a year later, as a monumental sculpture in Knokke/Le Zoute, Belgium, it allows real children to slide on its long tongue from its maw into the garden.

The dragon acquired another layer of meaning already in the 1960s. In a letter to Clarice Rivers, *Sweet Sick Sexy Clarice* (1968), who was the model for the *Nanas*, →Nana the monster stands for her friend's illness. In her drawing Niki de Saint Phalle literally tried to force the black-and-white dragon into a corner with positive, brightly colored personifications of her friend, combined with the advice simply to chase it away with concerted *Nana* power. In her educational book on AIDS,→AIDS she took up this metaphor again and had the dragon appear at the beginning, filling the image as the embodiment of the life-threatening illness, only to be chained up again at the end by her female alter ego.

E→ Emblem

Over the course of her work as an artist, Niki de Saint Phalle compiled her own collection of specific pictorial symbols, which she used in very different combinations. They could take on the character of ideograms, of pictorial symbols standing for single works, such as in a fictive letter to her daughter, Laura, in which the objects like a banana, an orange, and bread appear as drawn icons together with the corresponding terms.

In her tarot cards,→Tarot Saint Phalle's pictograms follow the tripartite division of art-historical emblem books with a main symbolic image, a title, and a comment beneath the figure. But the artist loosens up the reference of the three components that are supposed to establish the meaning of the image and make it legible. That opens up her symbols semantically and lends them multiple meanings. For example, on Tarot Card XIII, titled "Death," we see a drawing of a *Nana* on horseback and wearing a colorful cape. The figure's head is a skull, and she is holding a black scythe in one hand. The composite figuration of death and of life corresponds to the epigram beneath it, which in contrast to the title reads: "Death card NO. XIII MEM. There is no death—There is change—transformation. Our life is Eternal."[5]

In her "likes and loves" tableaus, in which Niki de Saint Phalle listed her penchants, interests, and inspirations, she ultimately developed a kind of mega-collection of personal emblems. The headline reads "I like, I love, I have been inspired by,"→pp. 23–24 followed by decoratively arranged visual symbols that use the allover principle with handwritten terms added. The loose arrangement of the pictograms on the white sheet lends them the status of words and sentences of a personal visual language. The overall edifice of title and drawings does indeed make sense, even if only a purely additive one. Because "I love" can be supplemented with more and more emblems, and the list of them could continue on additional pages. The emblems of animals, colors, artists, states of mind, flowers, landscapes, and films exceed all possible categorization and yet remain coherent to the extent they derive from Saint Phalles's self and her predilections.

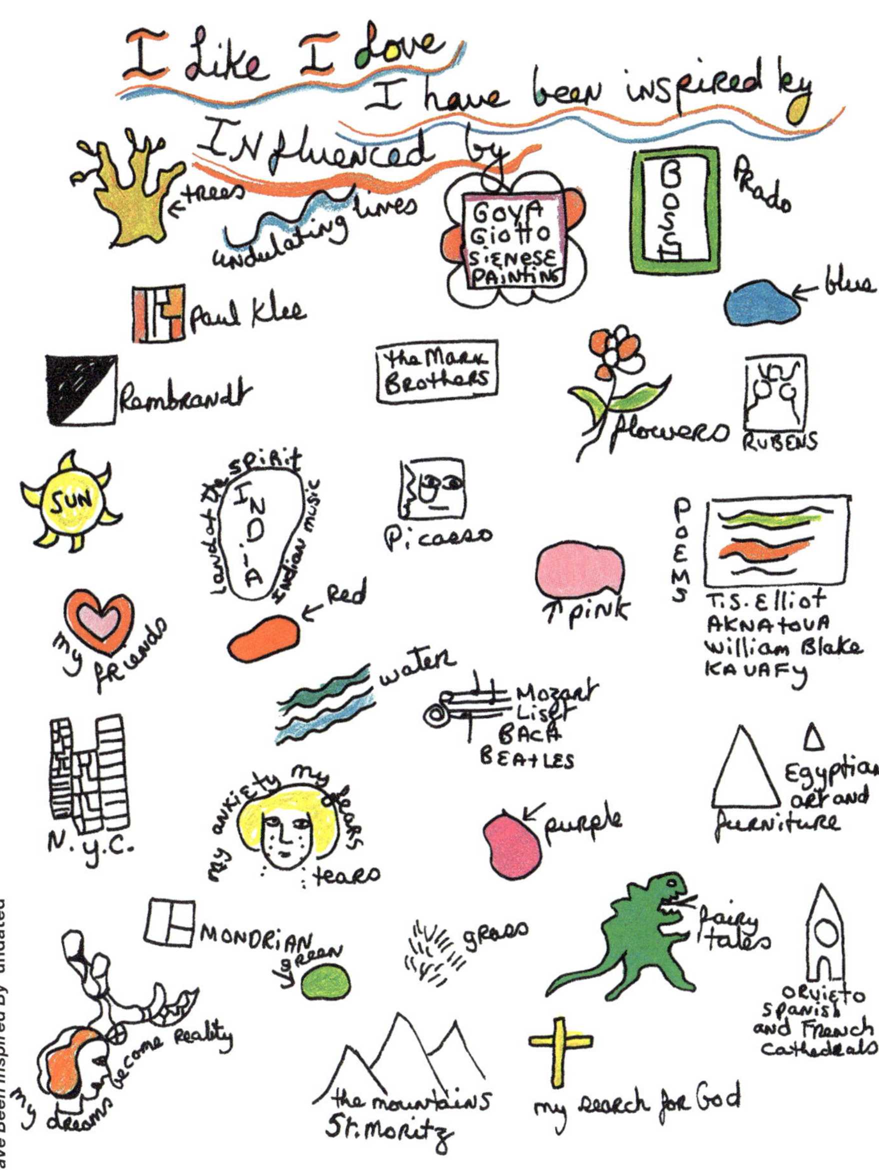

I Like, I Love, I Have Been Inspired By undated

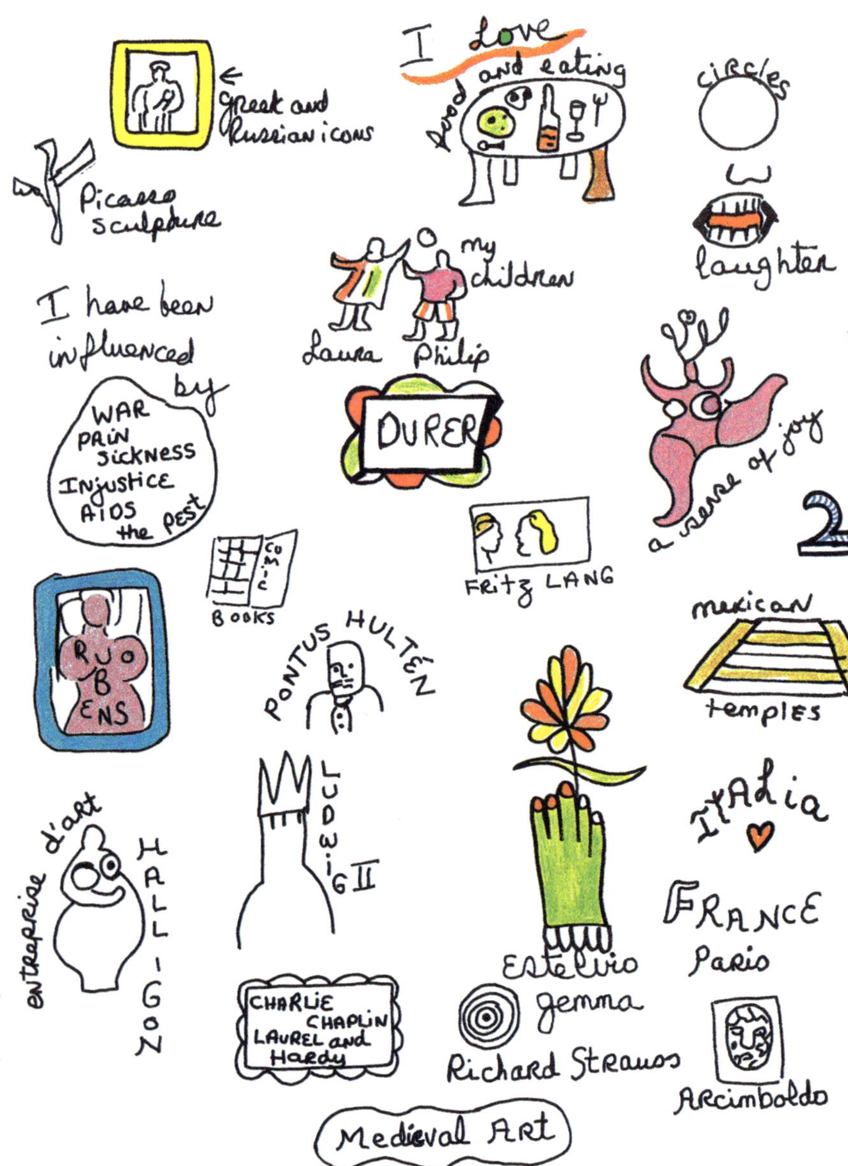

I Like, I Love, I Have Been Inspired By undated

By developing her own emblems, Niki de Saint Phalle created the persona of a woman artist whose emphatic relationship to the world can be expanded infinitely and whose diversity and unconventional interplay of her individual preferences we cannot capture in a single image.

MOVIES FORMED my ideas about love

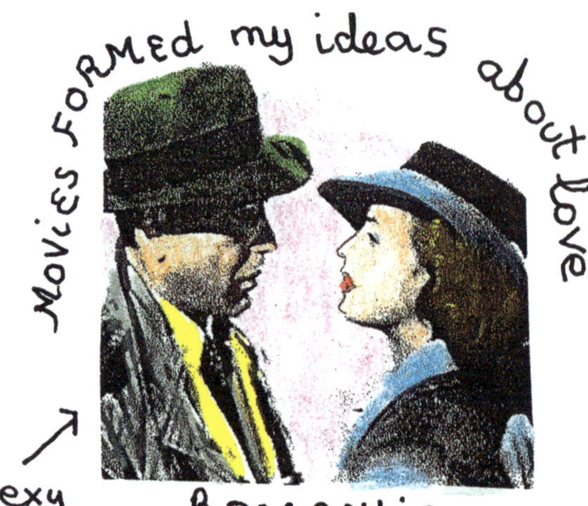

sexy ROMANTIC

HARPO was my first love

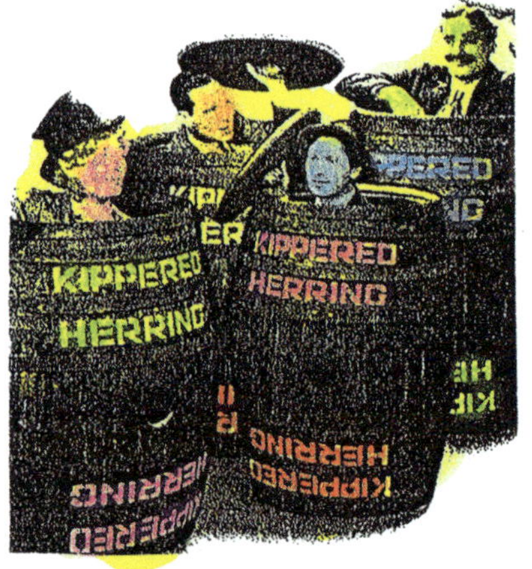

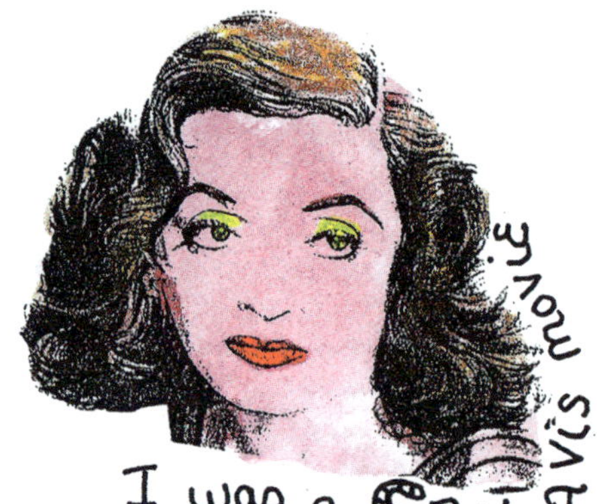

I was a FAN
I saw every Betty DAVIS movie

F→ # Film

Niki de Saint Phalle was an artist with an enthusiasm for film. Her memoirs, *Traces*, begin with a memory of the film *Rashomon* (1950) by Akira Kurosawa, which she saw when she was twenty and which in retrospect raised important existential and artistic questions for her. The film shows three different perspectives on the rape and murder of a young woman. Saint Phalle asks: "Which version was true? All of them? None of them?"[6] There are undertones of her uncertainty about her own memory of being abused by her father. But even more than that, the film opened up for her fundamental reflections on the relationship of individual and reality, subjectivity and the particularity of perception. "Where does that put reality? Does it exist?" she asks, "Do I exist? Is life a dream? My dream that I can choose to make a nightmare or a song?"[7] From her elemental cinematic experience with *Rashomon*, Saint Phalle gained great freedom to express herself from a radically personal perspective and create her oeuvre like a mosaic without solid cohesiveness or claim to universality.

Niki de Saint Phalle's enthusiasm was wide ranging; she did not distinguish between Hollywood and Nouvelle Vague but rather surrounded herself with her favorite films and actors and actresses: Humphrey Bogart and Ingrid Bergman appear alongside Harpo of the Marx Brothers and Bette Davis in *Traces*, and Charlie Chaplin, Laurel and Hardy, and Fritz Lang meet in her "Loves and Likes." Films were like music, art, eating and drinking, friendships and love the lifeblood of the artist. This is revealed most succinctly in Saint Phalle's interior design of her *Great Goddess* →Hon in Stockholm, whose gigantic body also housed a cinema.→p. 4

Niki de Saint Phalle pursued her pleasure in the moving image,→Kinetics expressed both in her dancing *Nanas* and in her collaboration with Jean Tinguely,→Jean Tinguely by making her own films as well. The motivating factor was the unexpected death of her father in 1967, whose sexual abuse of her when she was eleven years old she had not come to terms with and with whom she had not reconciled. With help from the British filmmaker and writer Peter Whitehead, she made the film *Daddy* in 1972–73, in which she celebrated a wild, sexually liberated world of women with exalted theatrical appearances of figures from her own visual cosmos, including mothers giving birth and the shooting artist. The whole film served to express in art her revenge against her father: "I gave free rein to my fantasies, and a mad anger arises from this film. Through the images, I trample on my father, I humiliate him with all my might, and I kill him."[8] That is even more true of her second film, *Un rêve plus long que la nuit* (*A Dream Longer than the Night*, 1976), which she made in 1975 with support from Tinguely → Jean Tinguely and the participation of many friends. In it, giant papier-mâché penises explode and men fight deadly duels with machines replacing their sex organs. In both films, the anarchic principle and the demonstrative artificiality of the figures and scenography dominate, which the artist uses to mock the phallocracy; a lesson that she might have learned not only from the Dadaists but also from Groucho and Harpo Marx.

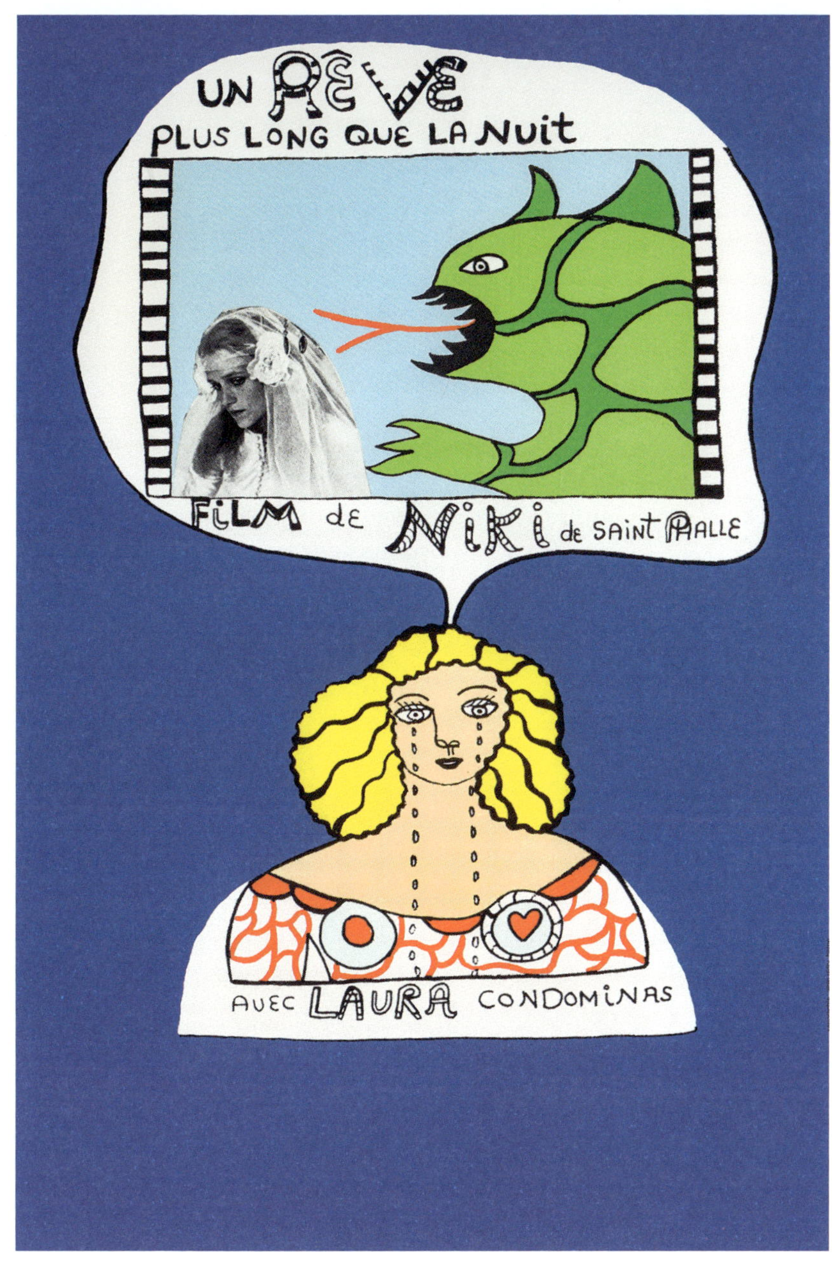

Un Rêve plus long que la nuit (A Dream Longer than the Night) 1974 screenprint 65.3 × 42.1 cm

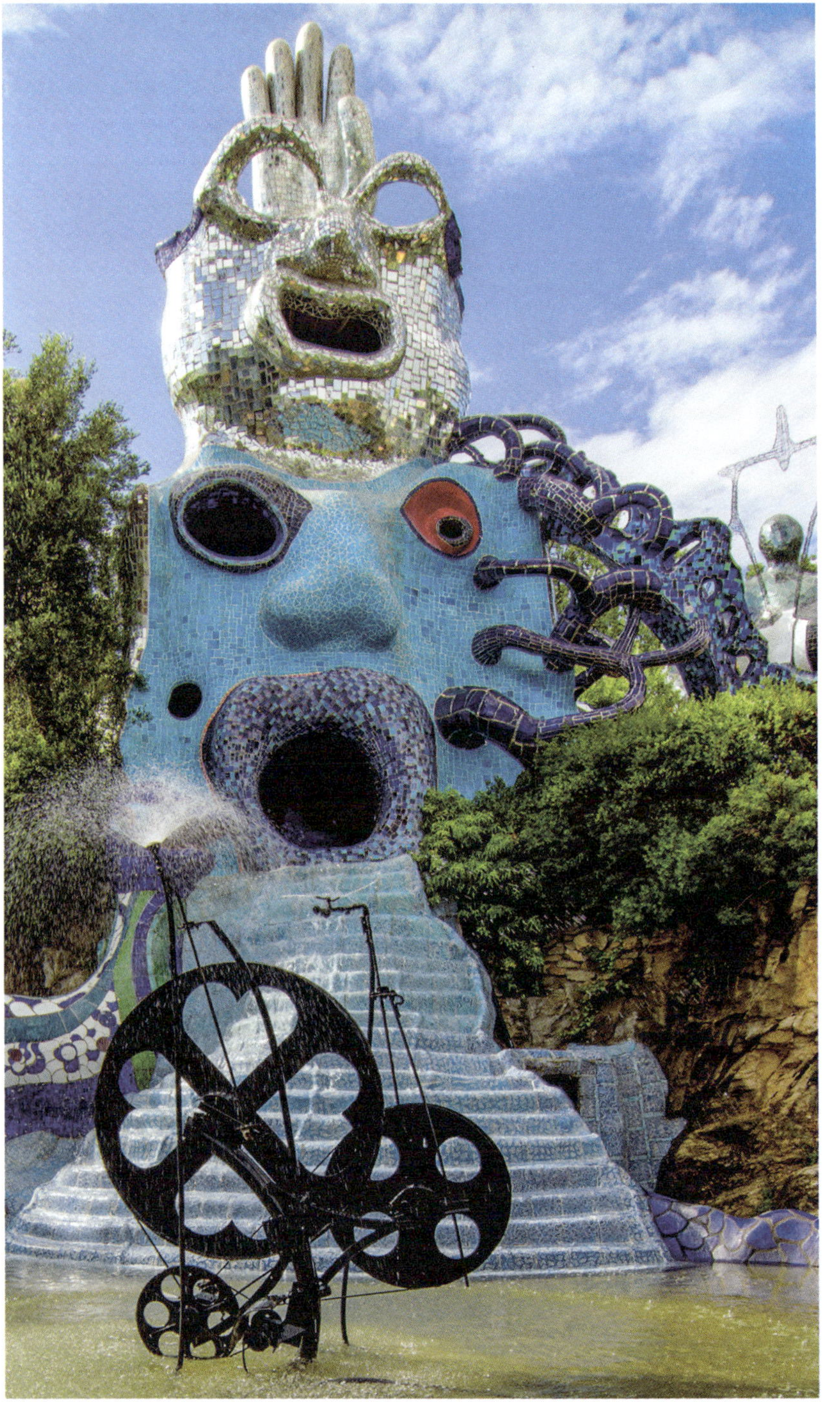

Jean Tinguely's *Wheel of Fortune* at the *Tarot Garden* Garavicchio, Italy

G→ Garden

Gardens are built dreams of paradise. They transform nature into landscape, plants into ornaments, animals into fauna, and people into demigods and lovers. The structure of their paths follows the narration of fairy tales: from station to station, visitors experience the surprising, the wondrous, and the challenging. For Niki de Saint Phalle, the garden is a model for a paradoxical experience of time: it offers simultaneously the promise of eternity and that of transformation.

In her *Tarot Garden* →Tarot in southern Tuscany, built from 1979 to 1998, Saint Phalle materialized the "dream of her life."[9] From 1950 onward, she had the idea of constructing a remote place inhabited solely by figures from her own imagination, in which art and nature would intermingle, each in its own way.

The great epochs of imagined and built gardens provided inspiration for her *Tarot Garden*: antiquity with its mythological descriptions of idyllic Arcadia and its imagined gardens of love,[10] examples from the Renaissance and the Baroque such as the Boboli Gardens in Florence or Bomarzo north of Rome, with their relics from antiquity and grotesque figures, and the English landscape park that imitated nature and replaces the geometric paths of its precursors with curving "beauty lines." The most obvious inspiration is that of Antoni Gaudí's Park Güell in Barcelona, with its large, organic, mosaic figures.

Niki de Saint Phalle's *Tarot Garden* lives from inversions: the *hortus conclusus* (enclosed garden) as a space closed off from the outside becomes her real model for an introspective perspective and at the same time the symbolic site of unbounded fantasy. Its twenty-two large sculptures based on tarot cards and decorated with colorful mosaic and mirror stones can be seen from a great distance but do not reveal their secret knowledge. Because they can be entered and inhabited, Saint Phalle transforms the sculptural into the architectonic and brings the natural symbolism of the grotto to the earth's surface. The idea of the *hortus conclusus* is transformed into the form of cloisonné, which determines the layout of the *Tarot Garden*. The individual figures are hedged in by trees, bushes, or shrubs. In contrast to mosaics, however, where gaps between the sharp-edged parts allude to a lost whole, here nature mediates between the parcels, allowing the sculptures to oscillate together with the vegetation. Her *Tarot Garden* is a manifesto for the meandering line and for polymorphous, opulent forms, → **Polymorphy**, → **Opulence** that invites sauntering and strolling for pleasure.

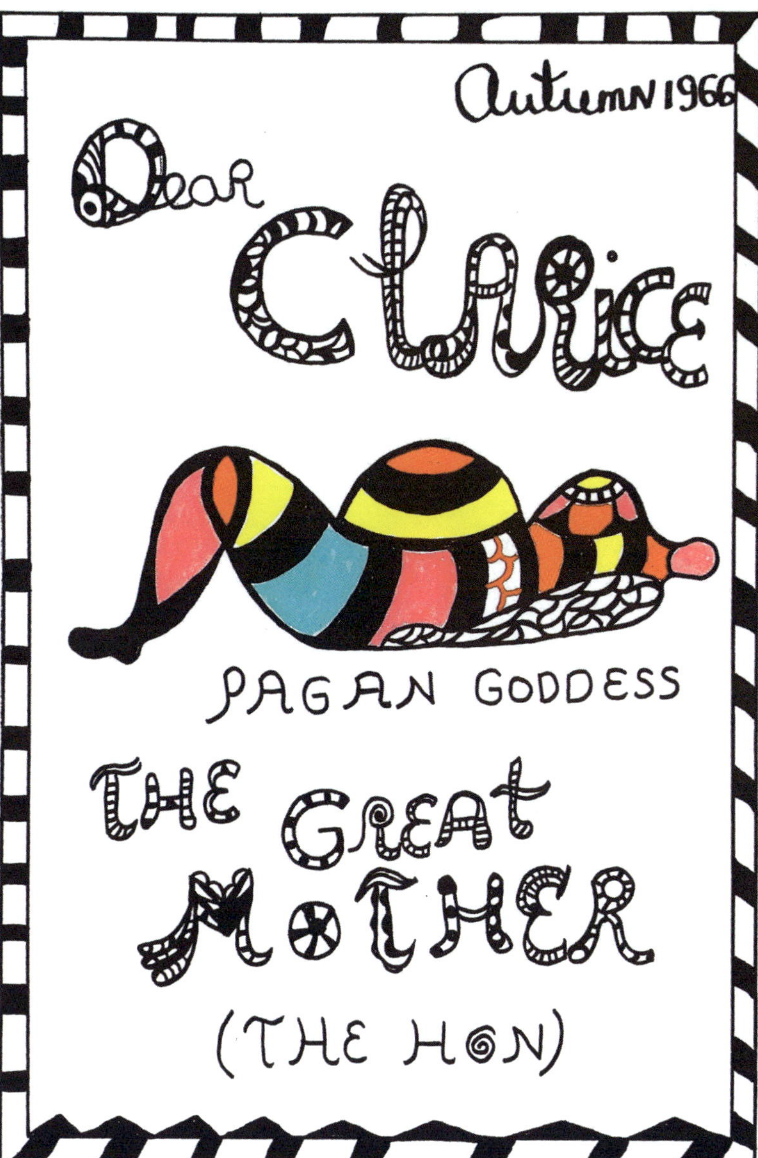

Dear Clarice 1991

H → # Hon

In 1961, the American artist Larry Rivers and his wife, Clarice, moved into the Impasse Ronsin → Impasse Ronsin in Paris, where they met Jean Tinguely → Jean Tinguely and Niki de Saint Phalle. Following her early assemblages and shooting events, → Shooting the artist began to take an interest in the plastic, curved forms of the female body. When Clarice Rivers became pregnant in 1964, Saint Phalle and Larry Rivers produced a sketch of her for which he drew the outlines and she filled them in.[11] Whereas in his first drawing Rivers presented the fetus in the womb in the tradition of anatomical illustrations, Saint Phalle covered the pregnant woman's body with a dense collage of colorful ornaments and emblems. → Emblem The inside and the outside merge into an artistic, multiform and multicolored membrane that celebrates the entire female body. With this allover principle, she negates the medical gaze focused on the reproductive organs and returns to the pregnant woman her outward attractiveness. Niki de Saint Phalle explicitly described Clarice Rivers as the model for her *Nanas* → Nana and the gigantic sculpture *Hon* (Swedish for "she"), also known as *Great Goddess*: "As you, Clarice, were the original Nana, consider yourself the model for the *Great Goddess*."[12]

In 1966, the Swedish curator Pontus Hultén asked Jean Tinguely, Martial Raysse, Claes Oldenburg, and Niki de Saint Phalle to build a large-scale sculpture for the eleventh Europarat exhibition at Moderna Museet in Stockholm. Instead of Raysse and Oldenburg, they were joined by the Finnish artist Per Olof Ultvedt. Inspired by Hultén's idea of a large-scale, walk-in *Nana*, they started their work. The large sculpture was titled *Hon: En katedral* (She: A Cathedral) and combined the dome structure of a Christian church with two spires and the ur-image of a woman giving birth as sign of matriarchal energy. Niki de Saint Phalle produced the maquette, and together the group designed the walk-in structure and the functions of the interior. The finished large sculpture is a *Nana* on her back with legs splayed at an angle. Its horizontal orientation made it possible to fit the *femme maison* into the museum space. The most astonishing thing for viewers was the entrance into her interior.

Niki de Saint Phalle and Larry Rivers *Clarice* 1964–65 collage, color pencil, pastel, graphite and ink on paper 156.5 × 112 cm

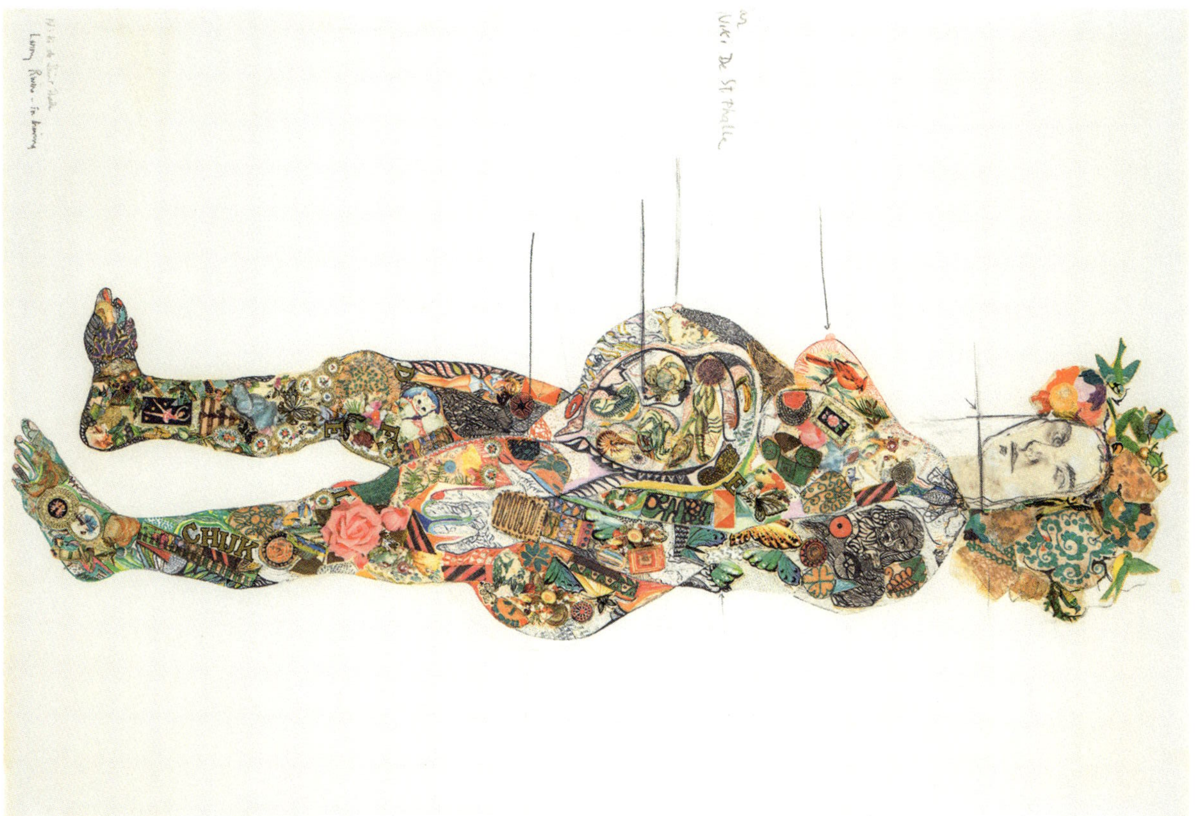

Between her opened legs, the green-and-black-painted gate of her vagina invited them in. The entry was chromatically integrated into the multicolored →Chroma painting of the whole, with her tumescent belly in red, her trousers in green and pink, and her garters in black. That stripped the entry of its spectacular quality, so that it had no pornographic notes whatsoever. The opening seemed rather to embody the encouraging "step right in" of the carnival barker.

And awaiting the public inside was indeed a series of entertainment stops on several levels that would have done justice to any fairground. In her left arm was a cinema, which showed a slapstick film →Film with Greta Garbo in her debut performance;[13] in her left breast was a planetarium, in her knee a red velvet sofa for lovers, from which one could view a gallery of forgeries. In the intestinal tract, a machine by Tinguely crushed the bottles being emptied in the milk bar of the right breast. In place of the heart, a moving sculpture by Utstedt set the rhythm, and in the left thigh a slide welcomed children large and small. In the middle of the dome of the belly was a viewing platform from which one could look out over the colorful mountains and valleys of *Hon*. Panorama and navel gazing became one in a humorous way at this culmination point.

Visiting the *Great Goddess* became a regression in the literal sense: returning to the womb.→Regression It offered the public an uninhibited visual pleasure that addressed all the senses and was not subject to any physical or aesthetic norms.→Opulence

In a tour de force, the artists built *Hon* in six weeks. In the three months before it was dismantled, the *Great Goddess* received 100,000 visitors,→p.4 who were charmed by it: "Everyone who saw her broke into a smile."[14] →Laughter

hon

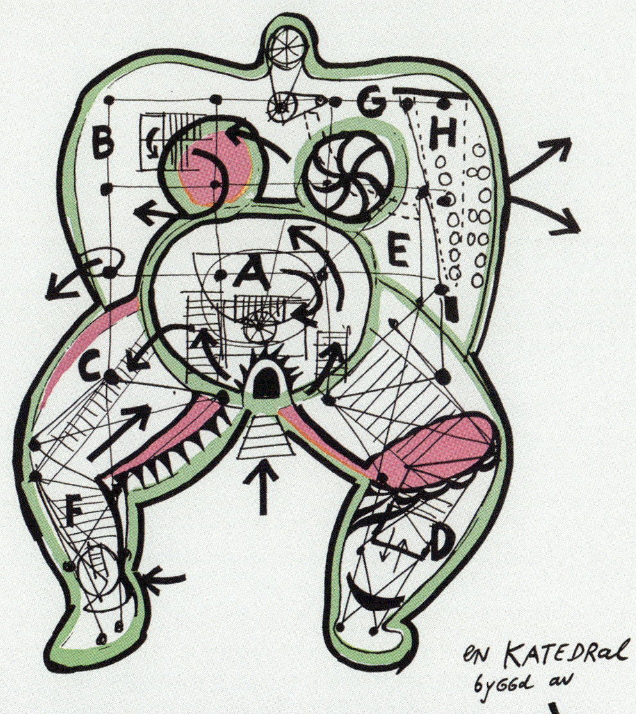

Moderna Museet

Alla dagar 12-17
Onsdagar 12-22
Efter 1/7 alla dagar 12-22

Niki de Saint Phalle
Jean Tinguely
Per Olof Ultvedt

Hon, *Moderna Museet, Stockholm* 1966, poster 100 × 70.3 cm

I→ Impasse Ronsin

The Impasse Ronsin, a cul-de-sac located between the rue de Vaugirard and the rue de Sèvres in the Parisian neighborhood of Montparnasse, was a special place in Niki de Saint Phalle's life and work. When she moved from Majorca to Paris in 1955 with her husband at the time, the writer Harry Mathews, and their two children, she initially worked in their spacious live-in studio on the rue Alfred Durand-Claye. Through their mutual friend the American metal artist James Metcalf, who had a studio on the Impasse Ronsin, they came into contact with many of his colleagues, such as Daniel Spoerri and Yves Klein, Larry Rivers and Robert Rauschenberg. They had their storerooms and workplaces there, where they often lived. "The studios were wooden shacks with tarpaper roofs, small windows, coal heating, limited plumbing and cold water only," she recalls. The "dilapidated shacks were nestled in an extensively overgrown tangle of garden, giving one the impression of being both in the middle of bustling Paris and in the rustic countryside at the same time."[15]

When Saint Phalle had the opportunity to take over Metcalf's studio for three months, she met the Swiss husband-and-wife artists Jean Tinguely →Jean Tinguely and Eva Aeppli. They lived and worked in a shack opposite the doyen of the Impasse Ronsin, Constantin Brâncuși, who had been living there since 1916 and became its central attraction. Whereas Tinguely was building strange constructions from disparate metal parts, Aeppli did charcoal drawings as well as life-sized female figures from fabric. This encounter with such disparate plastic and sculptural works of art may have caused Saint Phalle to make her first three-dimensional work that same year, which already featured the structure of her later works: a tree of plaster that she placed in front of the unused fireplace in her children's room and decorated with everyday objects.

In 1959, Niki de Saint Phalle separated from her husband and began her life as an independent artist. In October 1960, she and Jean Tinguely became lovers. She moved in with him on the Impasse Ronsin. A phase of mutual inspiration and close cooperation began, the first step and foundation for a lifelong friendship and mutual support.

The character of the Impasse Ronsin had already changed by the point. After the death of Brâncuși in 1957, many of the shacks were successively demolished, and his studio was dismantled in 1961 and rebuilt in front of the Centre Pompidou. Several of the artists used the resulting vacant lots for happenings. Saint Phalle was one of these, and her first *Shooting Paintings* were created there in 1961. If the Impasse Ronsin of the 1950s had been a place where artists, often male, met, now it was being used by women artists to break symbolically with the form of work-oriented creativity entirely. Saint Phalle's *Shooting Paintings* →Shooting established a tradition. On those same grounds in 1963, the young Argentinian artist Marta Minujín burned all of her works of the previous three years in a public action to protest academic conventions.[16] That event became the closure of an intense phase of creative collectivity. A new era had dawned, but the Impasse Ronsin was no longer its venue. Niki de Saint Phalle and Jean Tinguely left it that same year. In 1971, the last artist had to give way.

The artist settlement Impasse Ronsin in Paris

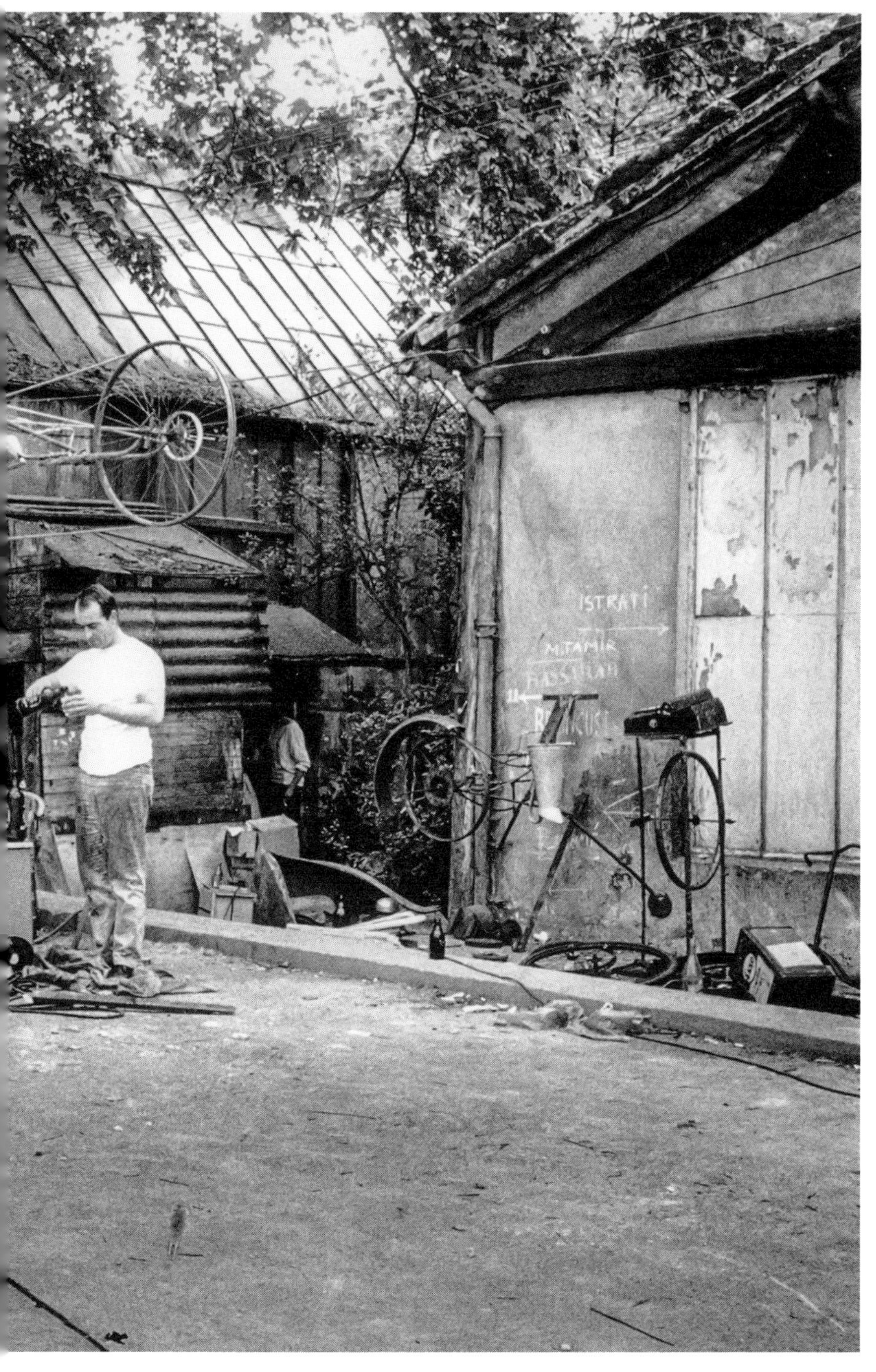
ISTRATI
M.TAMIR

J→ Jean Tinguely

Jean Tinguely was a Swiss artist in Paris and a Parisian by choice in the international art world. His assemblages from iron, which he often set in motion with motors,→Kinetics alternated between terrifying large machines and filigree webs. They reveal his country of origin: the home of clock handwork and of Dada. His early works, the *Méta-Matics*, were painting automatons that offered witty commentary on the myth of the artist-genius. The enormous painting machine he erected in the garden of the Museum of Modern Art in New York in 1960, which made hundreds of complicated movements, was equipped with a self-destruction mechanism that left only a few traces behind after thirty minutes. Tinguely then brought the parts back to the junkyard where he had gathered them. That closed a circle that symbolized the opposite of artistic productivity and at the same time reflected on the system of art. The unspoken motto was: he was not creating *l'art pour l'art* that will find its way into the museum's collection, but rather performing pyromaniacal circus magic that leaves nothing behind but junk.

This *Homage to New York* is symptomatic of many of Tinguely's later iron assemblages, with which he reduced the precision of the functional machine to the absurd and emphasized the playful quality of its gearworks.[17] When stripped of their purpose, they become meta-machines that do not open up a second level of meaning but indulge in a cheerful nonsense and a wild joy in destruction. The found pieces from which Tinguely assembled these works anchored his bizarre forms in the quotidian world. That made him a true member of the Nouveaux Réalistes in Paris and embedded his works in international Pop Art.

For Niki de Saint Phalle, Jean Tinguely was one of her most important artistic collaborators. They met on the Impasse Ronsin →Impasse Ronsin in Paris in 1955, were a couple in the 1960s, and until Tinguely's death in 1991 supported each other on many projects with ideas, materials, and artistic contributions. For example, Tinguely built iron pedestals for some of Saint Phalle's *Nanas*, constructed the welded frames for her larger-than-life sculptures, and during the financially difficult period of the *Tarot Garden* →Tarot, →Garden purchased many works from

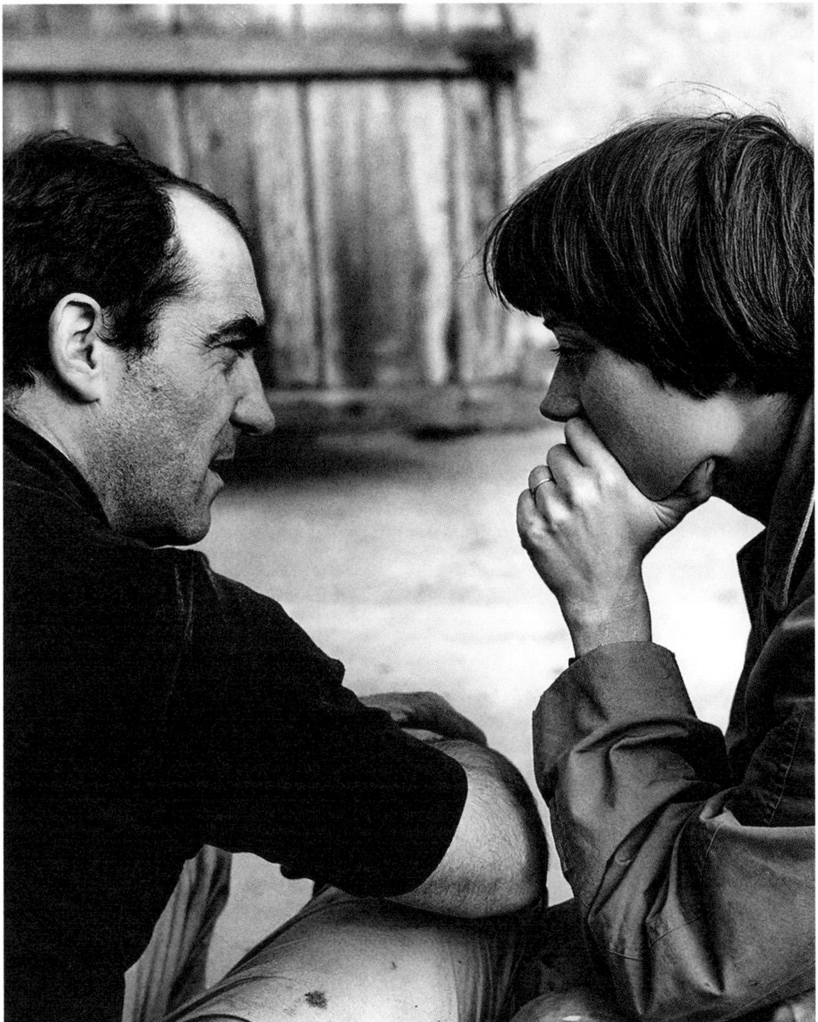

Jean Tinguely and Niki de Saint Phalle, Impasse Ronsin, Paris, April 11th, 1961

her so she could continue working on it. Saint Phalle, in turn, assisted him with his action in the desert of Nevada in 1961, *Étude pour un fin du monde II*, during which he exploded one of his gigantic meta-machines in reference to American nuclear experiments. She also supported him in his decades-long work on *Le Cyclop*, an oversized head in Milly-la-Forêt, near Paris, which she covered with one of her reflective mosaics.

Like his compatriots Hans Arp and Sophie Taeuber-Arp, Jean Tinguely cooperated with Niki de Saint Phalle on an egalitarian level as well: for example, in the case of the walk-in figure *Hon*,→Hon her *Le paradis fantastique* on the roof of the French pavilion during the Expo in Montreal in 1967, and the Stravinsky Fountain →Kinetics next to the Centre Pompidou in Paris.→pp. 90/91

As personalities and in their positions as artists, Jean Tinguely and Niki de Saint Phalle were complete opposites. Their joint works derived tension and wit from that. At the same time, in their cheerful, anarchic manner they were extraordinarily similar to each other, which is why they were called the "Bonnie and Clyde" of the art world.[18]

Niki de Saint Phalle continued with her cooperation with Tinguely even after his death. Her generous donation of his works provided the core of the collection for the Tinguely Museum in Basel. In a long letter to the deceased artist, she clarified once again their life together in order to go her own way in the end: "Now the time has come for me, Jean, to think about myself," she writes. "I am sure you are watching me, happy that I am taking new risks, continuing with the same enthusiasm."[19]

K→ Kinetics

The kinetic principle works in two ways in Niki de Saint Phalle's oeuvre: as a depiction of dynamics and as mechanized movement of her figures. The first form is inherent in many of the *Nanas;*→Nana the second is best developed by her figures in the company of the motorized sculptures of Jean Tinguely →Jean Tinguely in the Stravinsky Fountain in Paris.→Water Fountain →pp. 90/91

Whereas the devouring mothers →Mothers seemed to be paralyzed by a lethargic gravity, and even the reclining *Hon* →Hon was mainly characterized by her impressive groundedness, the artist let her *Nanas* dance again and again. Their corpulence and their conically pointed limbs gained a specific function in their movements. The curves of their bellies, their breasts, and their behind guide the viewer's gaze around the figures. Ring-shaped ornaments often help get our gazes circling around the *Nanas* as well. Volume and decor thus dynamize our perception and set us in motion prompting us to walk around the *Nanas*. Their feet, which often taper conically, add another kinetic effect. They seem to be balancing on one leg like ballerinas dancing *en pointe*. We think them capable of making a pirouette at any moment or of rising up in a perfect *élevé*. With their outstretched arms, they jubilantly escort this prospect of complete weightlessness.

When these dancing *Nanas* are standing on pedestals, they recall the figurines on old music boxes that delicately spin to the music. In Niki de Saint Phalle's collaborations with Jean Tinguely, this model becomes reality, albeit on a very different scale and with the mechanisms exposed. In the ensemble titled *Le paradis fantastique*,→p. 47 shown on the roof of the French Pavilion during Expo 67 in Montreal, several of Saint Phalle's monumental sculptures, including three acrobatic *Nanas*—doing the splits, riding waves, and doing a headstand—joined with Tinguely's *méta-mécaniques*. His constructions of blackened metal moved their wheels and joints mechanically. They were exposed motors without housings whose point was to demonstrate their kinetic principles.

By contrast, Niki de Saint Phalle's *Nanas* embodied a completely different principle of movement. They did not move, but instead represented the movement resulting from an innate physical impulse. One could see the loaded energy and body tension with which they performed their acrobatics. Yet like the best dancers among the *Nanas*, they had an inherent legerity signaled by the effortlessness and joy of their movements. The kinetic principle of Saint Phalle's sculptures was pure representation in comparison to Tinguely's sculptures. They did not move themselves. In their interplay, however, both positions emphasize this contrast and affect their counterpart. Tinguely's delicate-looking frames were addressing Saint Phalle's well-rounded figures, working against them, pressuring them, or lifting them into the air as a male dancer does the prima ballerina. The struggle of two principles of movement transitioned imperceptibly into a partnership.

Niki de Saint Phalle added a metaphorical level to *Le paradis fantastique*, which since 1970 had been permanently installed in the garden of Moderna Museet in Stockholm. "It represented our lover's battles together," she writes, "his black menacing machines were attacking my colored, rounded world. The two poles met—masculine feminine, black and color, movement and stability. It was a war without victors and vanquished."[20] The battle of the sexes illustrated in its contrasting figures and dynamics was for Saint Phalle an animated game between equals: a perpetual motion machine.

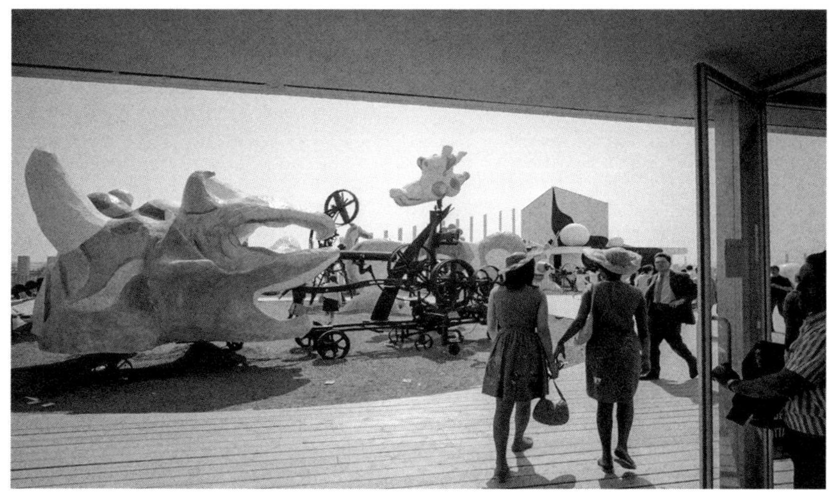

Jack Metzger **Montreal, Expo 67, rooftop of the French Pavilion** ***Le paradis fantastique*****, by Niki de Saint Phalle and Jean Tinguely**

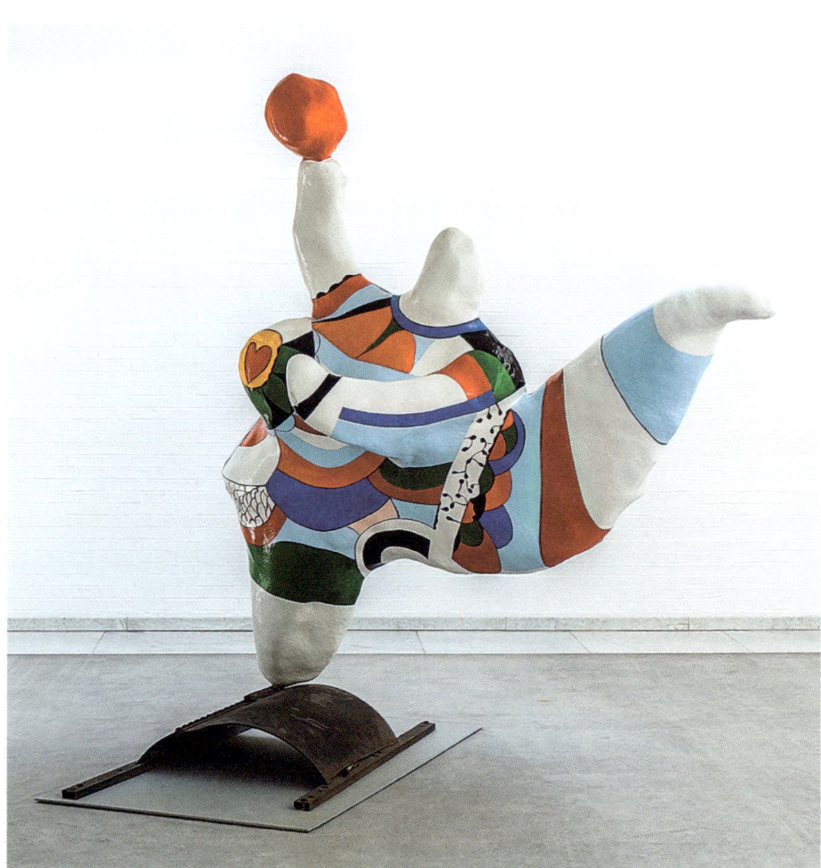

Nana au ballon 1971

L→ Laughter

Laughter liberates, laughter relieves fears, laughter prevents aggressions, laughter provides distance from oneself and from others. Niki de Saint Phalle loved laughter. In one of her *Likes and Loves* drawings, we see the emblem of an opened mouth and two rows of gleaming teeth and a red tongue next to the word "Laughter." It is closely related to such role models as Charlie Chaplin and Laurel and Hardy.→Film But laughter as an effect has to be teased out. And for that one needs wit and, in the artist's case, visual wit. At least since the era of the *Nanas*,→Nana Saint Phalle's individual figures as well as many of her constellations of figures have that.

One instrument of wit is intensification and exaggeration. Niki de Saint Phalle's figures of animals, people, and fantastical creatures play with that. For example, when her giant *Golem* (1972), based on a Jewish legend, on a playground in Jerusalem sticks out three bright red tongues from its maw that serve as slides, or the colorful snake in the Stravinsky Fountain makes a much narrower winding than reptiles in nature, we laugh at them and we lose our fear of them. This is true of the artist as well: "I think I was born with a terror of snakes," she writes. "Through making them, I have transformed my fear into joy. I have learned through my art to tame the things that scare me."[21]

The *Nanas* radiate the same wit as Niki de Saint Phalle's monsters. Unlike the latter, however, they provide an opulent →Opulence counterimage to society's dictate of the slender female body. Laughter results from the contrast that makes the standard evident in the first place. It does not denounce but rather emphasizes conversely what the dominant ideal lacks. Saint Phalle's *Skinnies* demonstrate that she is also capable of laughing at herself: filigreed forms of colorfully painted poles whose eyes, noses, and mouths are just as flat as their small breasts and their *vaginae dentatae*. The *Skinnies* reduce the female body to a silhouette that we literally see through. They are the counterimage to the voluptuous *Nanas* and their artistic exaggeration comments on the dominant image of women in just as humorous a way as their busty sisters.

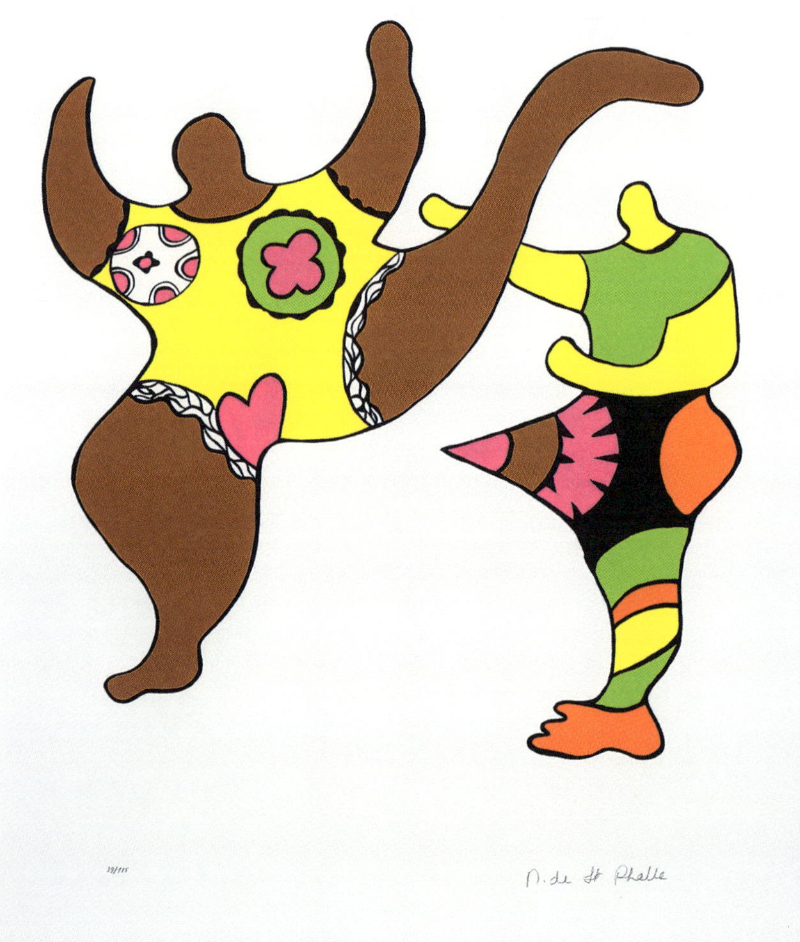

La Couple / La Danse from the series *Nana Power* 1970 screen print 76 × 56 cm

Nor does the relationship between the sexes escape Niki de Saint Phalle's wit. In a mixture of a parody of books on sex education and instructions for better sex, in one of her drawings she has a couple adopt a variety of sex positions. They over/do it in many respects. For example, the woman's genitals are dressed up as a heart; her behind as a red sphere; and her butt cheeks as ornamental circles. Nor does her partner's penis leave anything to be desired in terms of formal diversity: now a reversed ice cream cone, now a cylinder or a horn, it is always brightly colored and patterned in black and white. There seems to be no limit on the morphology of sex characteristics. They become objects and agents of the imagination. Two fictive protagonists are examples of this imaginary playfulness, living out their sexual fantasies or being haunted by them: out of the man's imagined image of a beautiful flower grows a colorful, erect cornucopia, while the serpent, as a symbol of dangerous seduction emerges from the hem of the black lace dress of a phallic woman.

The laughter about Niki de Saint Phalle's figures and their constellations is never at their expense. Her wit is always directed at the destructive structures that lurk behind people's hypertrophied imagination. In her work, the superhuman becomes the all-too-human. That makes her wit human and our laughter liberating.

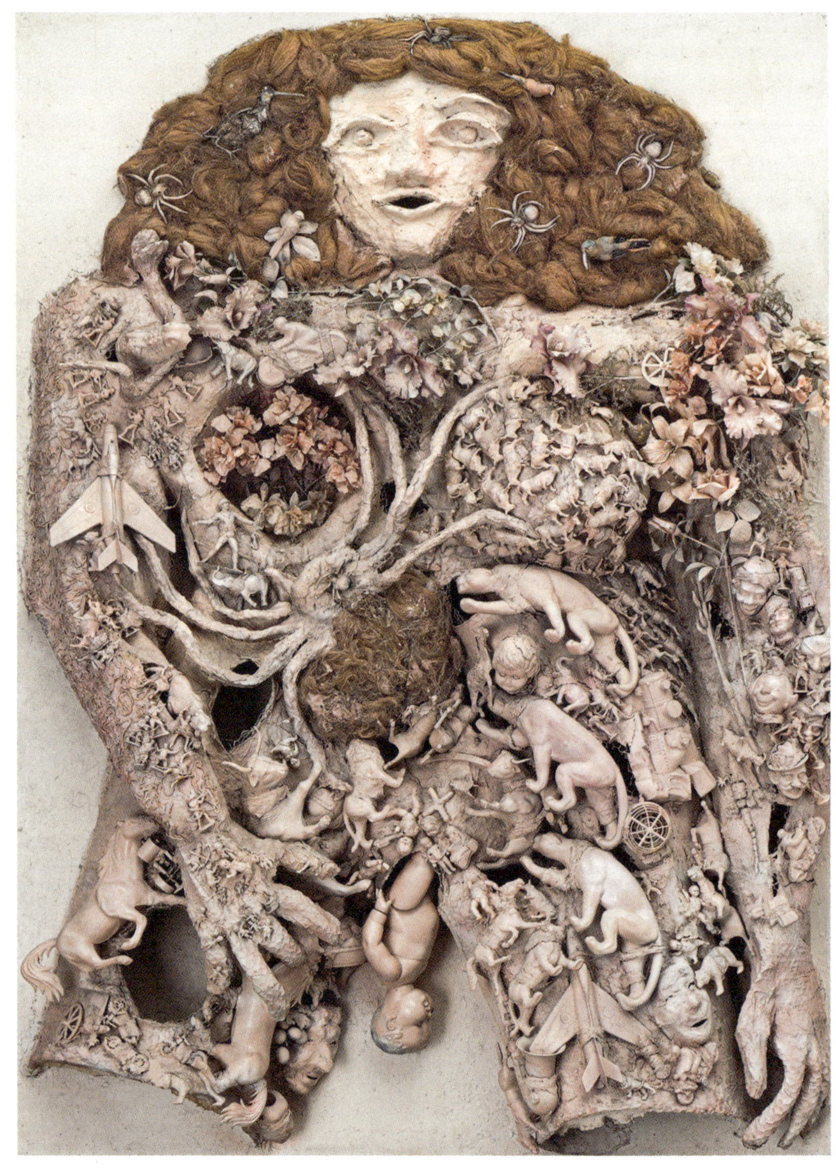

L'accouchement Rose (*Pink Birth*) 1964 paint, toys, various objects, mesh on wood 219 × 152 × 40 cm

M→ Mothers

In addition to her cheery *Nanas* →Nana and the larger-than-life *Hon*,→Hon whose corpulence personified both physical reproduction and artistic creation, Niki de Saint Phalle also thematized the dark sides of motherhood. "Evil mothers" occur in two phases of her oeuvre.

In the 1960s, we find them in the series of female figures in papier-mâché, which, like the *Brides*,→Bride also included mythical representatives of a destructive power. The inside of these witches, enchantresses, and goddesses is turned outward. Militaristic toys and doll babies, snakes, scorpions, and plastic skulls burst out of the monochrome crust of the epidermis. The entire body produces monsters. The mothers giving birth do not, however, suffer the corrosion of their epidermis but turn the permeability of their grotesque bodies into a force that produce the unimaginable. The doll baby borne by such a powerful mother with legs spread becomes one creature among many. Physical motherhood as supposedly the highest fulfilment of a woman is thus relativized. The female assemblage figure with her plastic newborn represents a deeply ambiguous figure: she embodies a brimming, uncontrollable, physical, and phantasmatic productivity and at the same time introduces only a stillborn and insignias of destruction into the artificial world from which she too is constructed.

In 1971–72, *Les mères dévorantes* (*The Devouring Mothers*) appeared in Niki de Saint Phalle's universe for the first time. On the occasion of an exhibition at the Gimpel Fils gallery in London, she had sometimes larger-than-life sculptural figures of staidly women appear with bodies deformed by voraciousness. They form narrative ensembles presented at the dining table alone or in pairs. Their food is even more astonishing: a small naked man and a crocodile are lying on plates. The appetite of the ladies seems to have no qualitative limits either.

In parallel with the presentation in London, Niki de Saint Phalle published a book titled *The Devouring Mothers*.[22] In size and form,[23] it imitates a children's book or notebook, and in the artist's drawings the devouring mothers are integrated into the story of a little girl whose side they take against her molesting father. The elderly women resemble, like grumpy cannibals, the large sculptures of the *Devouring Mothers*. Here, too, they eat what they are served: men and monsters.

The title of the sculptures and book illustrations makes it clear that the figures represent Saint Phalle's own mother and her aunt. Created in the context of her film *Daddy*,→Film the devouring mother has a double meaning here: an accomplice of the father who covers up his sexual violation of his daughter and an assistant to the artist who avenges her spouse's abuse of their daughter by symbolically rendering him harmless by "incorporating" him. That is an inversion typical of Saint Phalle. She at once undoes the birth and shrinks the father to a harmless embryo inside the mother.

Niki de Saint Phalle does not by any means embrace these two ways that the mother is an accomplice. In her *Devouring Mothers*, she pillories the mothers not only by exposing the motherly rites of authority but also their mechanisms of repression. The artist thus understood the *Devouring Mothers* both as victims and "as the extended arm of the patriarchy, because they force their daughters into their role as girls."[24] In a letter after her mother's death, she writes: "I did not want to become like you, mother. You accepted everything that your parents taught you."[25]

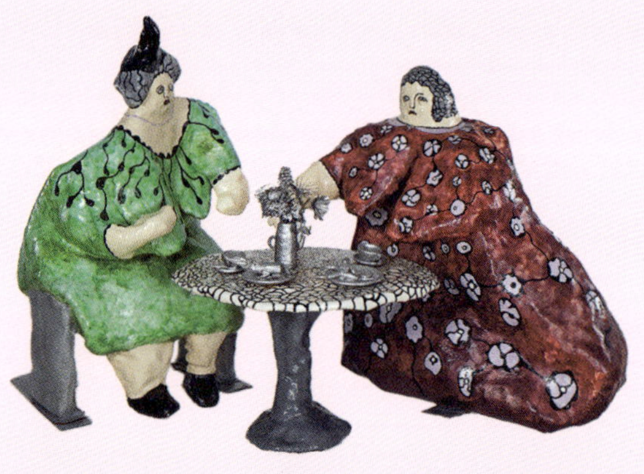

Tea Party, ou Le Thé chez Angelina (Tea Party, or Tea at Angelina's) 1971 polyester, painted

N→ Nana

The *Nanas* of Niki de Saint Phalle are her most famous works. We encounter them as gigantic monuments on public squares, as large sculptures in exhibitions, and as inflatable balloons; they can accompany us to the beach or as miniature statuettes standing on shelves in our homes.

They are characterized by their soft forms that result from the pliant material polyester, the chromatic choice of a colorful palette,→Chroma and an emphasis on the feminine curves of the belly and breasts, around whose gravitational field the head and extremities orbit like small satellites.

The *Nanas* are cheerful antitheses to the devouring mothers.→Mothers They radiate pure joie de vivre and send positive energy centrifugally into their surroundings. And they embody an ideal of feminine beauty that Niki de Saint Phalle deliberately tried to popularize through repetition to replace conventional ideas of femininity throughout the world. In 1967, she therefore titled her large exhibition at the Stedelijk Museum in Amsterdam *Les Nanas au pouvoir* (The Nanas in Power). In selecting that exhibition title, Saint Phalle was employing the rhetoric of the civil rights movements of the time with their slogans of love and freedom. With her *Nanas* she expanded those struggles against racism, colonialism, and capitalism to include the aspect of the battle of the sexes. She thus anticipated the agenda of the modern women's movement that was just beginning to take shape at the time. Saint Phalle's *Nanas* are anti-Twiggys, who countered the extremely thin, boyish supermodel of the Swinging Sixties with self-confident corporeal abundance by celebrating the female sex and the reproductive power of women. Today, the *Nanas* would be called body-positive and sex-positive because they not only encouraged tolerance of nonconformist physicality and insistent sexuality but also asserted themselves as omnipresent normality.

As a different ideal of femininity, Niki de Saint Phalle's *Nanas* had their very own lines of tradition. They are often said to be descendants of the so-called Venus of Willendorf: a limestone figure of the Paleolithic Age,

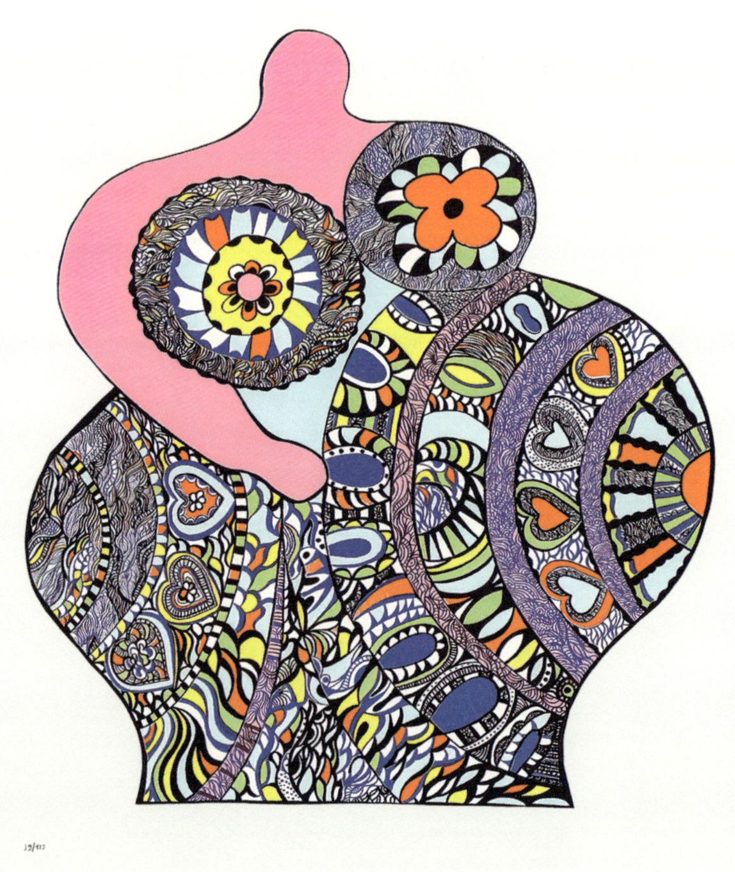

Nana Millefiori from the series *Nana Power* 1970 screen print 76 × 56 cm

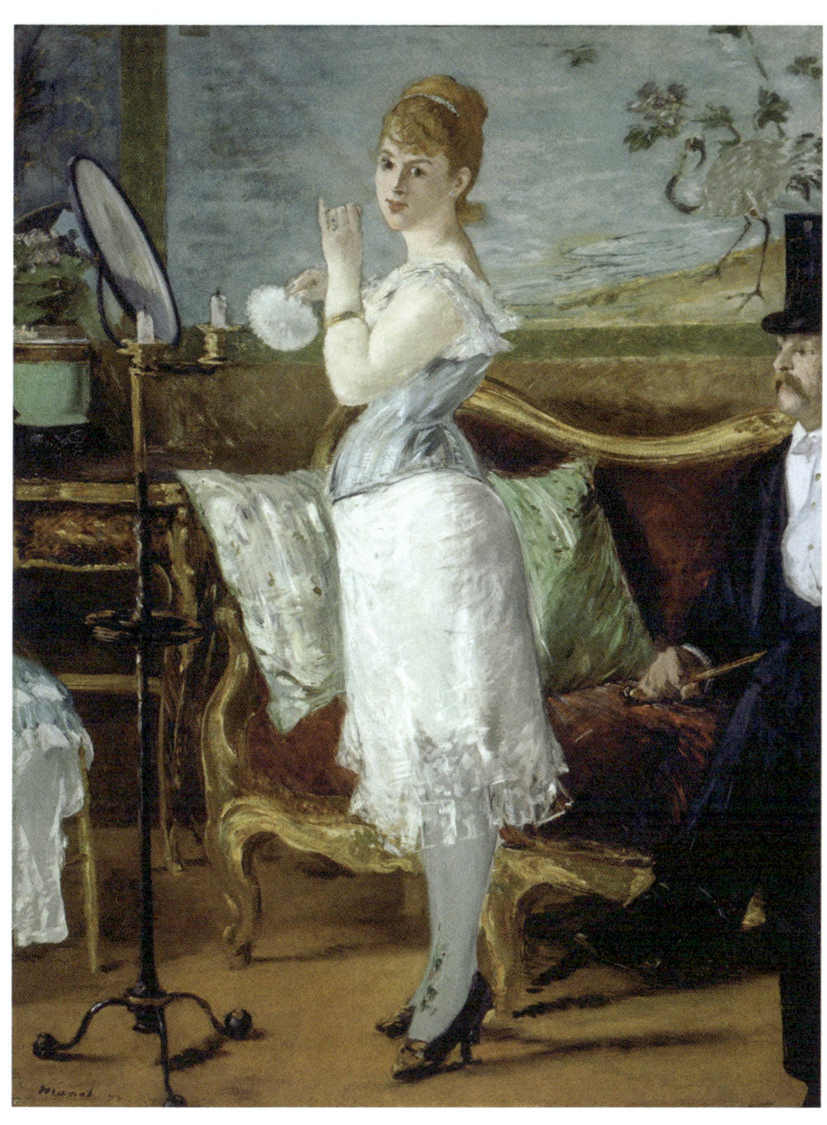

Édouard Manet *Nana* 1877 oil on canvas 154 x 115 cm

eleven centimeters tall and originally colored with red chalk, which has been interpreted as a fertility idol or depiction of a mother goddess because of her oversized breasts, belly, thighs, posterior,→Opulence and clearly defined vulva.[26] And, last but not least, there is their name, with which the artist established a connection to the Parisian courtesans of the nineteenth century. It is the name of Édouard Manet's famous depiction of a young mistress in her boudoir (1877),→p. 57 who self-confidently directs her gaze at the viewers, as well as that of the female protagonist of Émile Zola's eponymous novel (1880). It describes one of her theatrical performances: "Nana was nude. With quiet audacity, she appeared in her nakedness, certain of the sovran power of her flesh."[27] The same could be said of Saint Phalle's *Nanas*, except that they do not market their skin but instead self-confidently display their bodies as art.

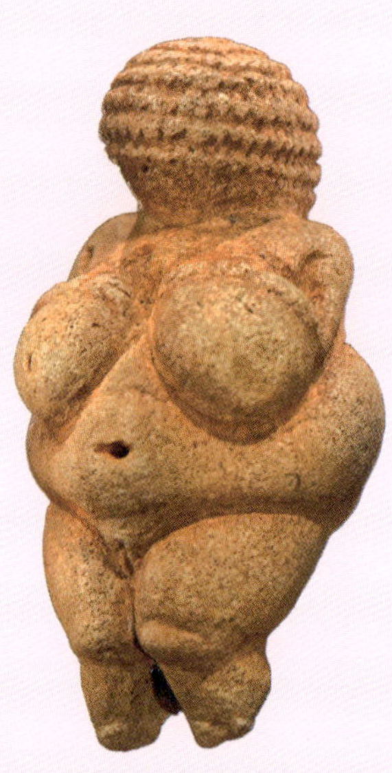

Venus of Willendorf upper paleolithic figurine

O→ Opulence

Abundance is not the same as quantity. It stands rather for a qualitative density that exceeds the necessary. Niki de Saint Phalle created sculptures of voluptuous bodies and drew on the abundance of her imagination. Opulence is therefore a signet of her figures and of her creativity.

The opulence of her figures since the *Nanas* →Nana is revealed in the excessive curves of their bodies that exceed a human scale not only in their size but also in their volumes. The bulges often appear in surprising places or in taboo zones of the body. They attract our eyes and become showplaces of transgression. The curves of the figures lend the bodies the potential of an unbounded wealth of form. But they never become amorphous in the process. The material polyester permits surprising expansions but at the same time keeps the ampleness in check. The opulent quality of her *Nanas*,→Nana *Hon*,→Hon and monsters →Dragon fulfills a function comparable to the grotesque described by Mikhail Bakhtin. It indicates on their bodies the carnivalesque break with norms and the limitations imposed by shame.[28]

Their colorfulness →Chroma and lush ornament adds a richness to Niki de Saint Phalle's figures that is entirely their own. Polyester lends great intensity to the colors and an abundant vitality to the decoration. The bright colors inscribe the principle of opulence directly into the surface of the figures. They accentuate and increase the diversity of forms.→Polymorphy Sometimes, however, the colors take on a life of their own as ornamentation that celebrates itself in effusive splendor.

For Niki de Saint Phalle, opulence is an essential basic principle of her artistic activity. She draws on the wealth of her imaginings. And she has so many of those that she generously gives them away. In several self-portrait drawings, she describes her ample imagination leaping out of her head: the fantasies literally grow out of and over her head in the form of wheels, snakes, or colorful tentacles. The separation between her outer face and inner vision is eliminated. That may frighten viewers, as with the head of the Medusa, but the artist's alter ego does not turn her imagination against us but rather empties out the cornucopia of her fantasies before us as a present.

This gesture of the gift is also under the sign of excess in Saint Phalle's work: she gives us not just her heart but also her breasts and her mouth, not just a thousand dollars but also her time, not just all her ideas but also her arts of cooking. The material and the immaterial come together in a humorous potpourri, but it never turns into an overwhelming potlatch.

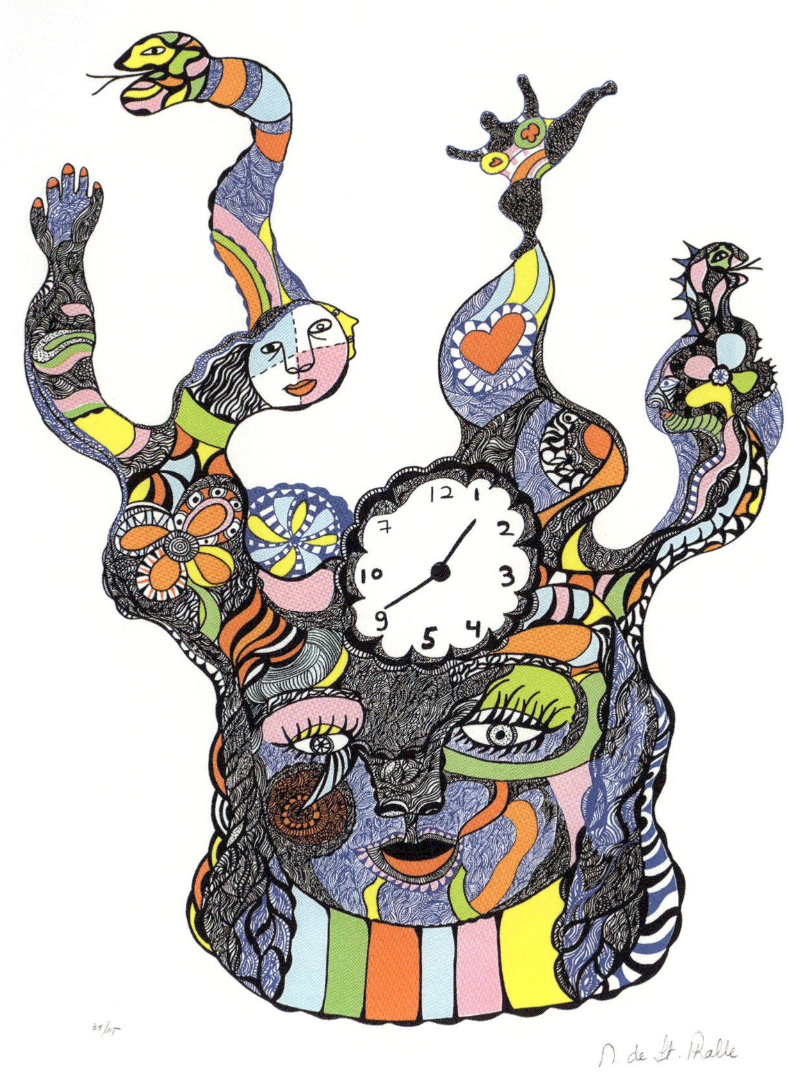

Clock Head from the series *Nana Power* 1970 screen print 76 × 56 cm

The Devil 1985 polyester, painted 260 × 225 × 110 cm

P→ Polymorphy

In addition to abundance,→Opulence diversity is another essential feature of Niki de Saint Phalle's figures. They can only rarely be reduced to a single, self-contained physical form. With their surprising curves and extensions, these figures stretch out expansively into the space surrounding them. Several of them even go a step further, in that autonomous morphological forms evolve out of them. The latter do not usually look as if they have been "applied" but rather like genuine outgrowths from a core figure that thus proclaims its potential to multiply its forms.

For example, out of the trunk of Niki de Saint Phalle's serpent tree a wreath of reptile heads grows in all directions. Their skulls of various sizes appear to be split up to the neck by their gaping jaws. The maws of the snakes with their red, black, or white color contrast with the heads and produce independent concave forms. The snakes' bodies also form the strong, pliable branches of the tree. Their colorful ornaments distinguish them from the monochrome heads. Together with the trunk and its nose-like roots, they convey an impression of a dancing figure multiplying its lithe arm movements. From this perspective, the snake heads look like gloves with which the puppet master of a Punch and Judy show presents the monster by opening and shutting its red mouth. The polymorphy of the serpent tree gets our perception flowing. We realize that a figure always has more than one view or meaning. And it makes us aware of the transformative power of our own imagination, which can turn the work of art into ever-new forms.

Niki de Saint Phalle also employs polymorphy in a humorous way →Laughter to undermine the polar opposition of the sexes. Her tarot figure of the devil unites many animals in one form: one leg has a hoof, the other a bird's beak; the head has a horn, the face a black goat's beard, and the wings are those of a bat. Geometric and rounded patterns of colors compete on the surface of this figure, whose silhouette is defined by its round, feminine hips and broad, angular shoulders, which transition into pointed wings. The artist deliberately gives the by no means demonic devil both breasts and a penis. Saint Phalle does not leave it at this hermaphroditic equipping of the incarnation of all evil; she does not simply add polar sex characteristics, she also transforms testicles and penis into gilded body parts with several erect outgrowths. It is reminiscent of an inverted udder. The diverse forms produce multiple meanings, taking the sting out of evil in a playful way and placing the devil on a pedestal as a cheerful god of polymorphous sexuality. Adam and Eve, who dance *en miniature* at his feet, appear barely to notice the anklet-like chain with which they are shackled to him.

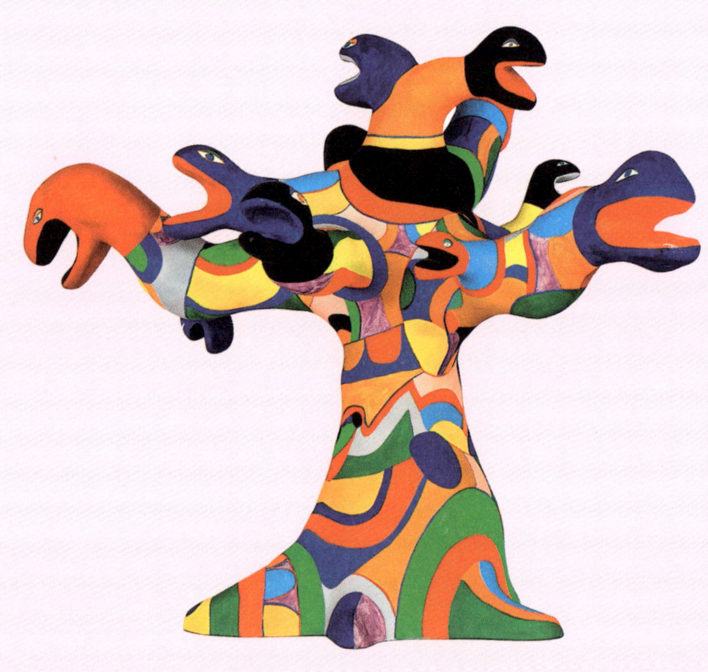

L'abre de vie (_The Tree of Life_) ca. 1974 polyester resin, painted, gold leaf, color pencil, pastel 65 × 52 × 42 cm

Q→ Queen Califia

Because the climate in Southern California did her damaged lungs good, Niki de Saint Phalle moved to La Jolla in 1993. Until 1998, she attended to the completion of her magnum opus, the Tuscan *Tarot Garden*,→Tarot, →Garden from there. At the same time, she became increasingly interested in California's multicultural art and history and began to look for a place to realize another sculpture garden. The city of Escondido in San Diego County made a space in Kit Carson Park available for her project. The city's name, which Spanish colonists had given to what had been an Indigenous settlement, means "remote, hidden." For Saint Phalle, it was a welcome opportunity to explore the traces of Indigenous, Central American, and Spanish traditions and myths: "Native American culture is an inexhaustible source for me right now, I read and watch films about it; I meet and speak with Indians. The oral tradition is still very much alive with them and it is the inspiration for my new garden."[29]

In 1983, Niki de Saint Phalle had previously designed a giant sun god for the campus of the University of California in San Diego, for which she adapted elements of Mexican symbolism. It would recur again later as an echo both in the tarot figure of the sun →Tarot, →Garden and the firebird of the Stravinsky Fountain in Paris.→Water Fountain The figure is an eagle, the animal of the coat of arms on the flag of Mexico, but it is not killing a snake, as it is on the flag. Rather, it welcomes all visitors to the university to enter through the gate on which it stands with legs spread. Its head is crowned by a golden diadem of rays like the one on the head of the Aztec sun god.

Elements of this monumental sculpture and the emblems on which it is based are also found in the garden in Escondido. The main figure there, however, is feminine, and its syncretism is derived from the sixteenth-century chivalric romance *Las sergas de Esplandián* (The Adventures of Esplandián) by Rodríguez de Montalvo. It is Queen Califia, a black Amazonian queen and ruler of the mythical island of California, who with an army of female warriors, a large fleet, and a flock of birds of prey fights on the side of the Muslims against the Christians who have occupied Constantinople. In Niki de Saint Phalle's

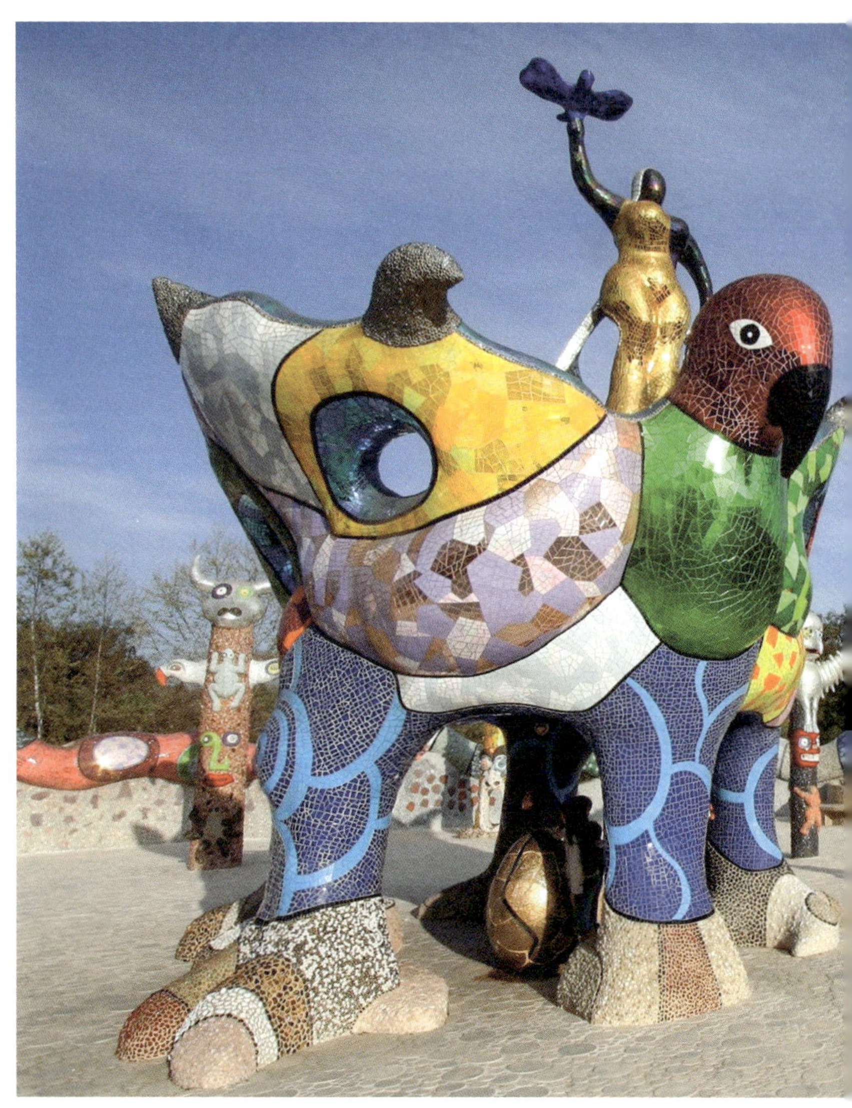

Queen Calafia's Magical Circle Escondido, California 1999–2003

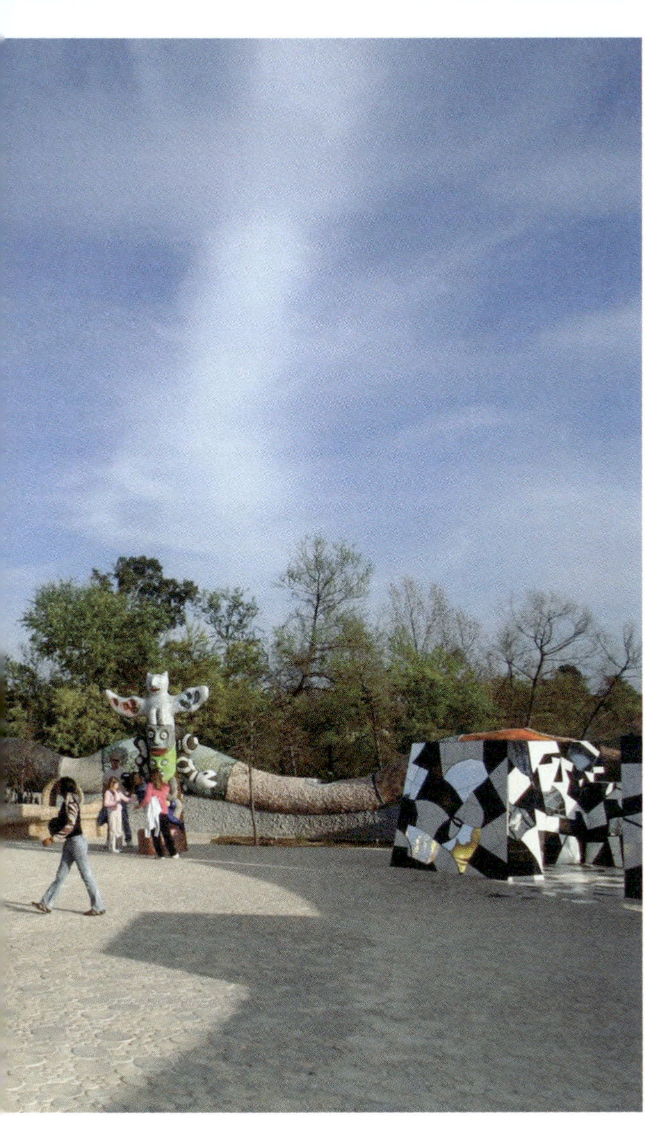

work, her realm is a *hortus conclusus* in stone. It is surrounded by a round wall, on whose wavy edge gigantic snakes with open mouths guard the terrain. A wall with angular black-and-white tiles initially prevents visitors from entering. Once they have arrived at the interior of the circle, they see before them a gigantic bird looming in the center on five column-like legs with the claws of a griffin. Its compact body is decorated with colorful mosaic stones, and its raised wings perforated by oval openings. Its enormous head rises above its glimmering green breast. Standing upright beneath the bird is a golden egg, like that of Columbus, serving as a fountain: water as the life-giving element and the egg as a symbol of origin are combined. The culmination, however, is the figure of Queen Califia standing on the gigantic animal's shoulders and posing like the Statue of Liberty. Her black skin contrasts with her gold dress, which exposes her left breast and shoulder. Her silver hair is divided like a double train in two strands that sweep back. From her raised right hand, a deep-blue bird rises into the air with wings outstretched. The queen is surrounded by eight totems whose emblems combine Native American, pre-Columbian, and Mexican mythology into fantastic totems. The elements earth, air, water, and fire are assembled with the gods, demons, animals, and masks associated with them and form the positive archetype of California as a strong Black woman created by Saint Phalle. *Queen Califia*, however, is not only a mythical figure. The artist also saw her as an homage to the Hispanic and African-American population of the United States and as a political statement against George W. Bush's restrictive immigration policy.[30]

The powerful female figure Queen Califia personally tasked her with creating a temple in her honor, Niki de Saint Phalle wrote.[31] She was not able to complete the commission herself. *Queen Califia's Magical Circle* was accomplished in 2003, a year after her death, according to her instructions.

R→ Regression

Since the *Nanas* →Nana at the latest, Niki de Saint Phalle's oeuvre has repeatedly been characterized as cheerful and naive. The writing style of her artist's letters and books, derived from the writing of children, their vivid language, their direct address, and the simple form of their emblems,→Emblem which seem to have sprung from the realm of pure imagination, all suggest that interpretation. This apparent regression of form and content should not, however, be understood in the psychoanalytical sense of a reversion to the behavioral patterns of early childhood, but rather in the philosophical sense as a deliberate search for the origin and causes of things. Saint Phalle's specific recourse to forms of expression associated with childhood has its method. She employs it to ensure her emotions are the driving force of her creative work, to create her own cosmos inhabited by imaginary figures, and to obtain latitude for artistic action beyond pre-established conventions.[32] "Nature, dragons,→Dragon monsters, and animals have kept me in touch with the feelings I had about these things as a child," she writes in her memoirs. "I feel that the part of me that stayed a child is the artist in me."[33]

Niki de Saint Phalle thus elevates this "deliberate regression" to a programmatic level, giving her access to an arsenal of forms and motifs that predates the canon and is not subject to any of the rules of established art history and criticism. Moreover, regression as an artistic method enables Niki de Saint Phalle to create her own world in which the polymorphous →Polymorphy dominates and the real can be turned into the fantastic. This often results in humorous moments,→Laughter even when it is about serious things such as fear of illness, death, or the loss of love.

For example, in a farewell letter to Jean Tinguely,→Jean Tinguely the loss of a loved one is not really thematized as retrospective mourning about all things they will no longer be able to do together, even if the heading "My love we won't" might suggest that. Instead, the colorful emblems initiate an actualization of all the pleasant projects the two lovers undertook together or what they still had planned. The look backward is replaced by the present day. Our

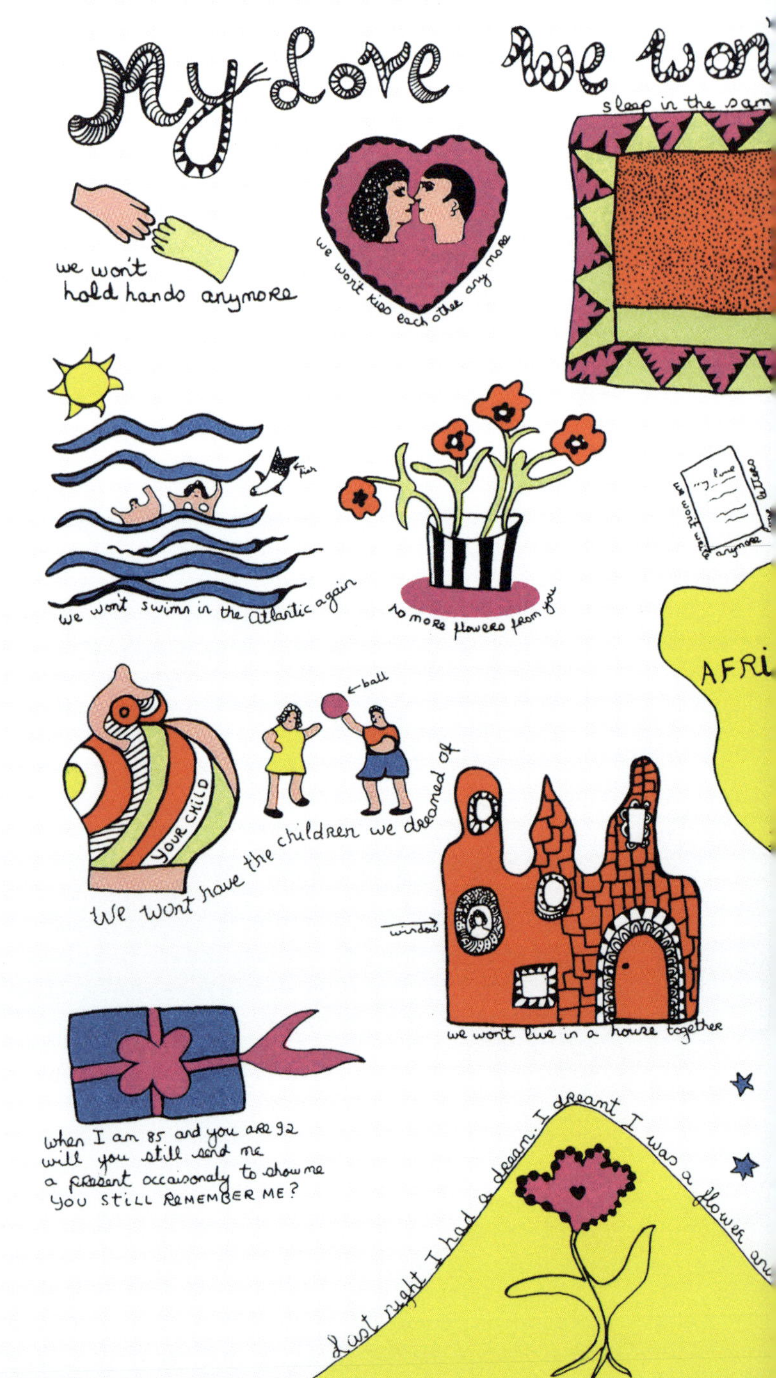

My Love We Won't 1968 screen print 49.5 × 61 cm

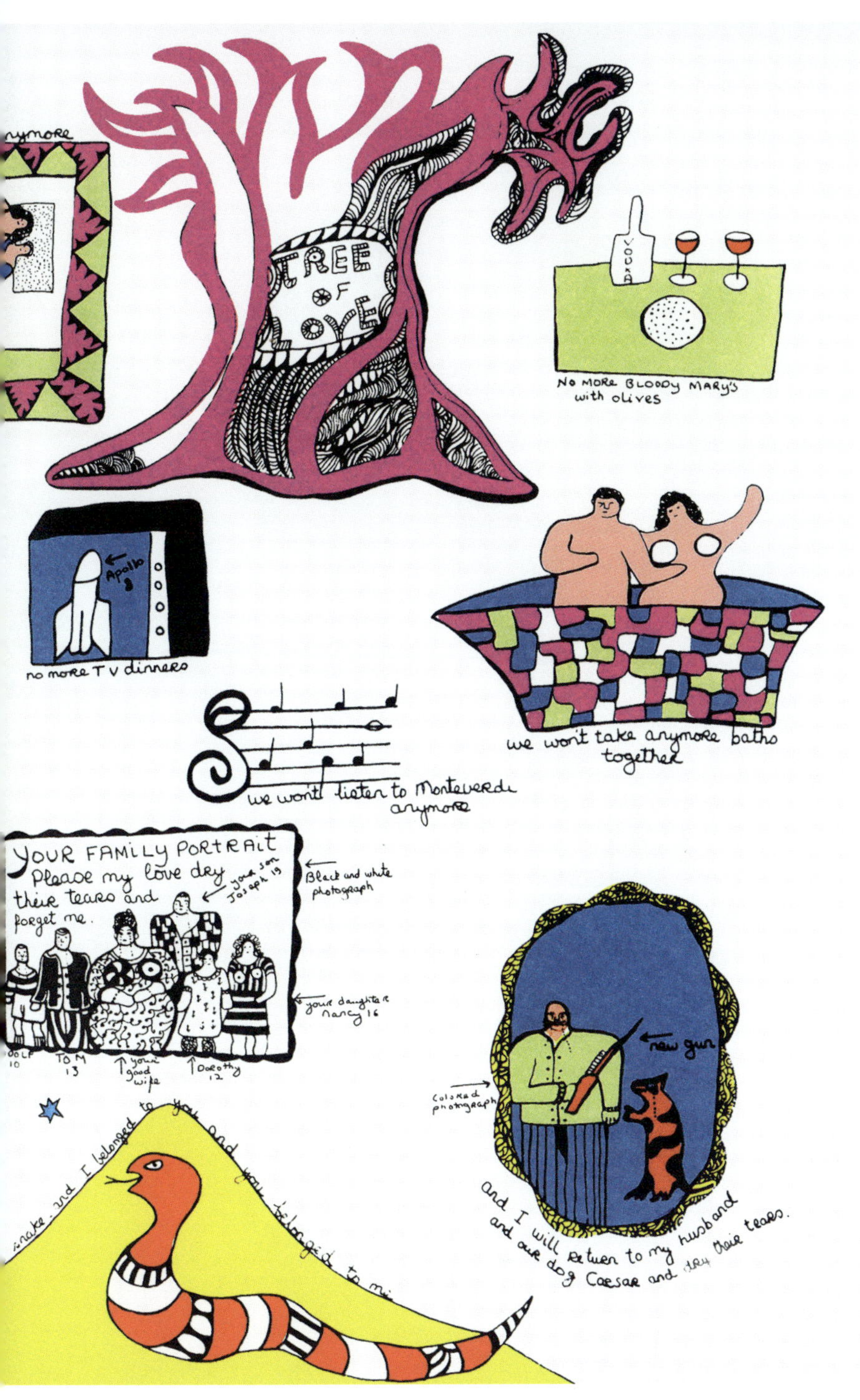
nymore
TREE OF LOVE
VODKA
NO MORE BLOODY MARY's with olives
Apollo 8
no more T V dinners
we won't take anymore baths together
we won't listen to Monteverdi anymore
YOUR FAMILY PORTRAIT
Please my love dry their tears and forget me.
your son Joseph 19
Black and white photograph
your daughter Nancy 16
OOLF 10
TOM 13
your good wife
Dorothy 12
new gun
Colored photograph
And I will return to my husband and our dog Caesar and dry their tears.
nake. and I belonged to you and you belonged to me

undisguised pleasure in the colorful emblems and small scenes turns the loss into a celebration of their relationship with all its pleasurable qualities. The "childlike" illustrations also manifest a confidence that emphasizes positive memories of their life together and uses them to motivate a different but happy future.

Saint Phalle employed the method of fictive regression in a similar way in her educational book about AIDS. →AIDS The deliberate use of "childlike" fantasies and the "infantilizing" of forms in general helped Niki de Saint Phalle to lessen the drama even of heavy themes without trivializing them, to focus on positive aspects without denying the dangers and losses, and to emphasize emotion without sentimentality.

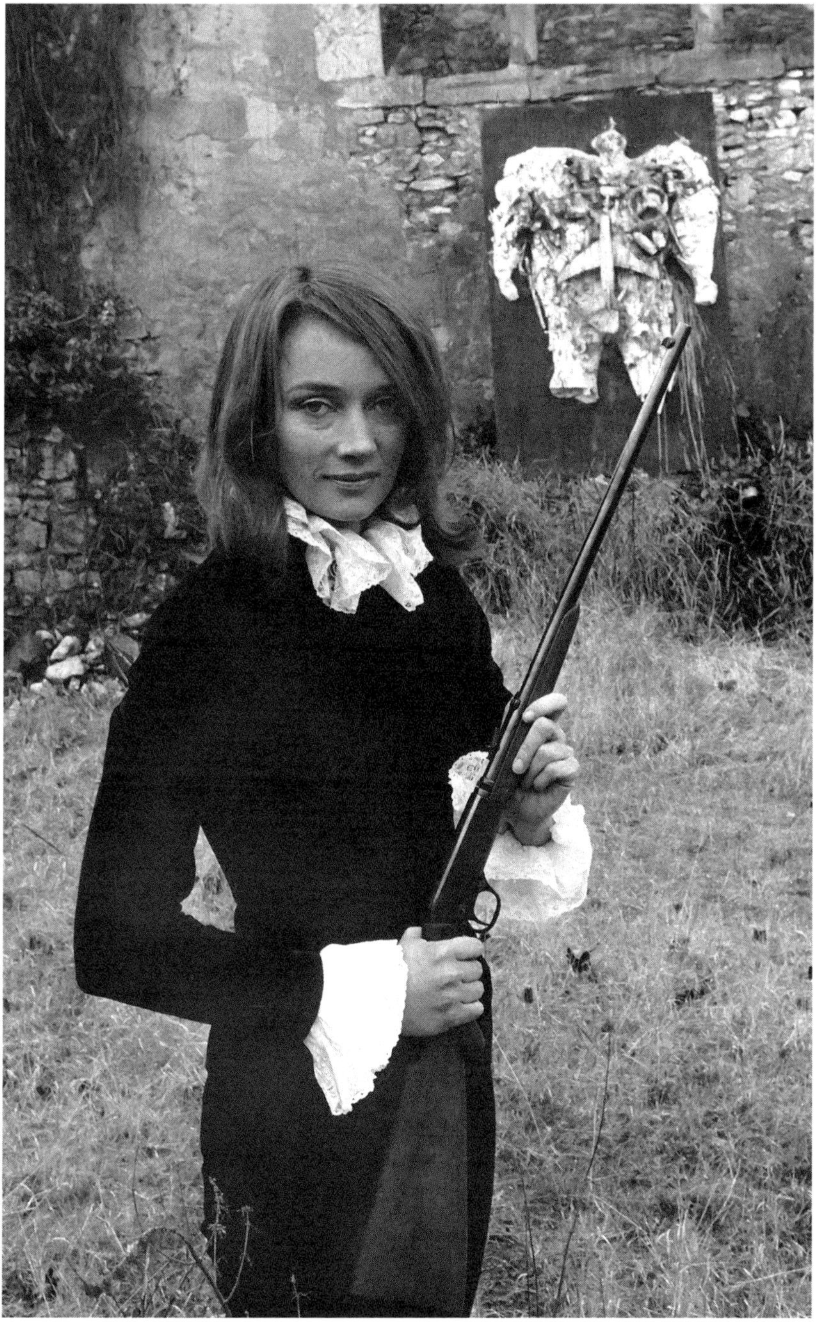

Niki de Saint Phalle in front of her shooting painting *La mort du patriache* (*Death of a Patriarch*) 1972

S→ Shooting

Niki de Saint Phalle's shooting events of the early 1960s, known as *Tirs* (Shootings), immediately made the young artist internationally famous. These happenings had been prepared by a transition in media in her oeuvre that occurred around 1959. After she had seen an exhibition of recent American art at the Musée d'Art Moderne de la Ville de Paris, she was especially enthusiastic about the *Combine Paintings* of Robert Rauschenberg, on whose canvases abstract passages interacted with everyday objects applied to them. Her encounter with younger artists on the Impasse Ronsin →Impasse Ronsin reinforced her will to break free of pure painting and turn to assemblage. She endowed seemingly innocent motifs of brides →Bride and mothers →Mothers with destructive toy objects such as pistols, knives, and rifles, and brought to light the physical and social violence they embodied. By integrating objects into her tableaus, Saint Phalle linked these fantastic figures to quotidian modern culture. Artistically, that brought her close to the Nouveaux Réalistes, an association founded in Paris in 1960 under the direction of the French art critic Pierre Restany. The collective's program was to reject the *l'art pour l'art* of Abstract Expressionism and Art Informel and emphasize the character of their works as objects and events as part of the real world.

That provided the backdrop for Niki de Saint Phalle's *Shooting Paintings*. Her immediate neighbors, Larry and Clarice Rivers, had initially been horrified by the artist's experiments with shooting on the vacant lot resulting from the demolition of Brâncuși's studio. The only wall that remained had been shared with the Rivers' studio. The artist also fired a small paint canon at her reliefs.[34] On February 12, 1961, however, Saint Phalle went public with her new work. She and Jean Tinguely →Jean Tinguely invited their friends to the Impasse Ronsin. She had mounted reliefs on the walls of one of the vacant lots that concealed bags of paint, eggs, and pasta. A rifle lay ready, and she encouraged the audience to use it to shoot at the assemblages. One by one, the guests followed her instructions, until finally the artist herself took up the weapon. The result was an art massacre: the surfaces of the works had burst in many places, and the content of the bags poured

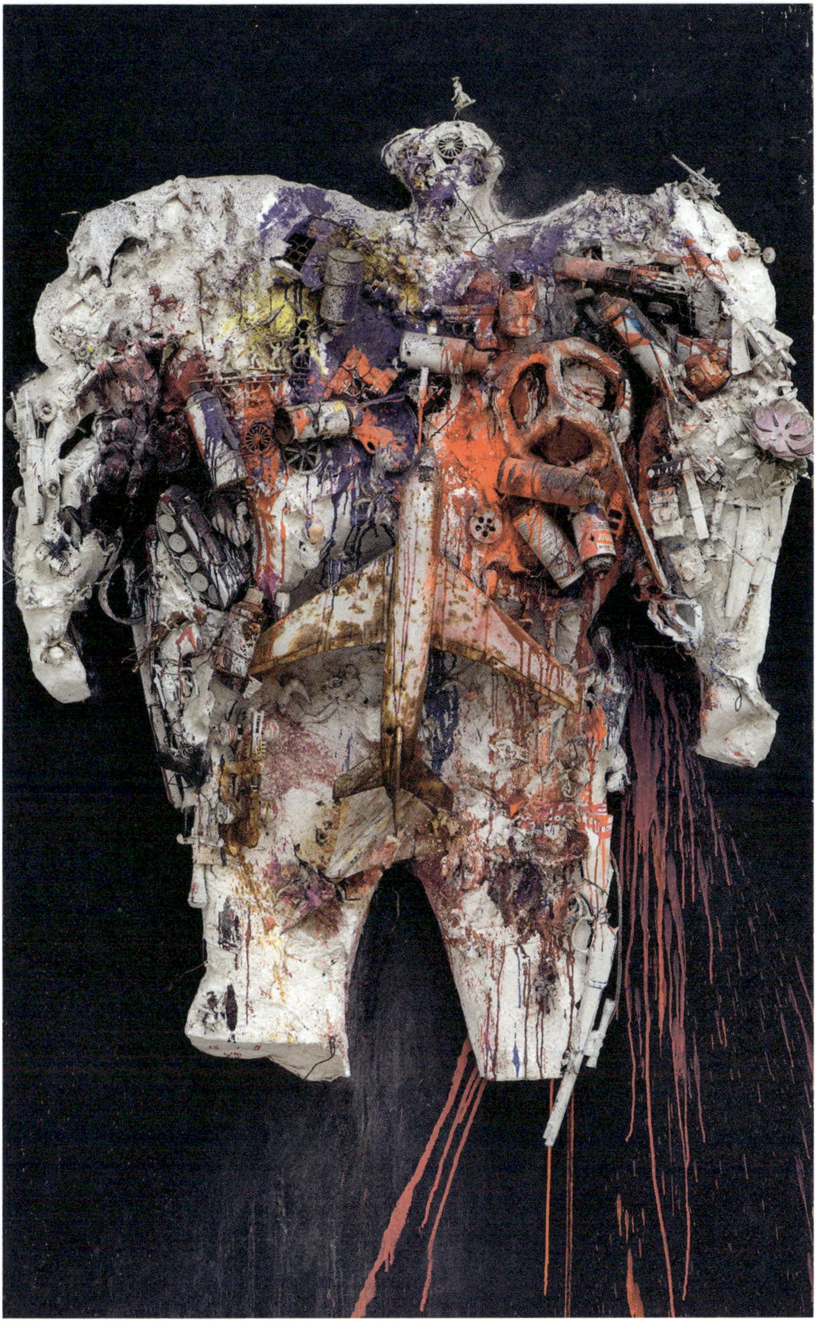

La mort du patriache (Death of a Patriarch) 1962 plaster, paint, various objects on wooden board 251 × 160 × 40 cm

out through the bullet holes for all to see, like intestines or fake blood. The colorful cascades brought the anemic white of the plaster reliefs to life in a disturbing way.→ Uncanny A symbolic transformation had occurred that played with the existential metaphors of life and death,→ Vanitas violence and rebirth, artistic action and the work's automatisms.

It had all the ingredients of mythologizing: a scandalous art event that was a kind of big bang of the art of the action and the happening; the ephemeral character of the action, which survives only through the filter of individual stories and in the fragmented moment of single photographs (by Harry Shunk and Jean Kender); a redefinition of the artist, the public, and the work; and it was initiated by a delicate young woman who presented herself as a modern Amazon.

Niki de Saint Phalle repeated her *Shooting events* many times. What had begun in 1961 with several such happenings on the Impasse Ronsin, she subsequently continued in a series of galleries and museums throughout the world. Increasingly, attention focused on the artist doing the shooting, who accordingly stylized more and more professionally in her outfit as a kind of artistic Emma Peel in a tight-fitting white or black pantsuit and tall boots. The participating guests were no longer primarily fellow artists but visitors to the gallery or museum. Consequently, the collective act of producing art gradually receded into the background and in the end what remained in the photographic documentations was the icon of the modern *femme forte* who had herself fired the starting shot for her international career with her spectacular actions.

T→ Tarot

The monumental *Tarot Garden* that Niki de Saint Phalle created near Garavicchio in southern Tuscany between 1978 and 1998 is her largest and best-known Gesamtkunstwerk.→p.30 Its precursors were Antoni Gaudí's Park Güell in Barcelona →Garden as well as the Mannerist park in Bomarzo with its fantastic monsters. Even more so, she had been inspired by the individualistic lifework of amateur artists such as the postal clerk Ferdinand Cheval, who from 1879 to 1912 built in Hauterives, France, a gigantic palace of lime, mortar, and cement with numerous figurines from biblical, Indian, and Egyptian legends, and Simon Rodia, who from 1921 to 1954 built enormous towers of junk and concrete decorated with shards in the Watts neighborhood of Los Angeles. Like those loners, Niki de Saint Phalle financed the *Tarot Garden* herself and thus preserved the freedom to design and implement her very personal mythology on a scale and at a pace appropriate to it.

Tarot cards have been used for games and prophesy since the fifteenth century. The tarot is a pack of twenty-two trump cards with symbols known as the Major Arcana, and fifty-six suit cards known as the Minor Arcana. Niki de Saint Phalle chose the Major Arcana and turned its traditional symbols into the drawings and large sculptures of the *Tarot Garden*. In the park in Tuscany, she arranged the figures as if laying out tarot cards. Visitors therefore walk through a gigantic interpretation of her fate as she herself saw it. The park can thus be understood as a three-dimensional, visual autobiography of the artist.[35]

Niki de Saint Phalle did not just create a monument to herself with her *Tarot Garden* but decided to live in the park for an extended time as well. She set up a residence in the right breast of one of the central figures: the Sphinx-like, monumental Empress (Tarot Card III). Like a womb,→Regression the interior of the figure becomes the artist's outer protection and at the same time the place from which she finished the rest of the garden with help from experienced assistants with whom she had cooperated on earlier projects and from local residents.

The intermeshing of inside and outside, power and danger, male and female characterizes the dynamic of the overall site. For example, the large sculptures can not only be viewed from outside, but they can also be entered, like the early monumental figure *Hon*.→Hon In contrast to Stockholm, however, here the surroundings are not the architecture of the museum and of the city but rather nature. Because the symbols of the tarot cards put the individual in a cosmic constellation, this is a logical spatial decision. The antagonism of the sexes is a theme of several of the configurations in the *Tarot Garden*. In a humorous way,→Laughter a bright-red, phallic rocket and the colorful tower of the emperor's castle with its gilded upper shaft are placed immediately adjacent to the Emperor (Tarot Card IV), or a man and a woman are shackled to the Devil (Tarot Card XV). As if in a summary of her oeuvre, in the *Tarot Garden* we encounter familiar figures from Niki de Saint Phalle's private emblems:→Emblem the lady taming the dragon is the symbol of Strength (Tarot Card IX); the firebird stands for the Sun (Tarot Card XIX); and a dancing *Nana* is balanced on an egg symbolizing the World (Tarot Card XXI).

Niki de Saint Phalle took great liberties with the details of the tarot. For example, she fused the first two symbols, the Magician and the High Priestess, into one configuration. As a symbol of intellectual and physical creativity, they unite the forces that distinguish Saint Phalle as an artist. The water spraying from the open mouth of this double figure sets the Wheel of Fortune (Tarot Card X) designed by Jean Tinguely →Jean Tinguely in motion.→p. 30 Right next to it, the transparent *Skinny* figure of the Fool (Tarot Card 0) strides across the water. Saint Phalle explicitly identified with the fool,[36] since only those without preconceptions, like children and fools, are capable of experiencing the world as a miracle. That is also Saint Phalle's message to the visitors: only those who do not try to interpret every detail and allow the garden to keep its secret will gain surprising insights: "If life is a game of cards," we read at the entrance to the *Tarot Garten*, "we are born without knowing the rules. Yet we must play our hand."[37]

TAROT CARDS

THE CARDS

If life is a game of cards,
we are born without
knowing the Rules.
Yet we must play
our hand.
Is the tarot only a
card game, or is there
a philosophy behind it?

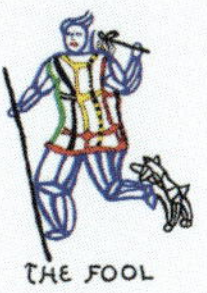

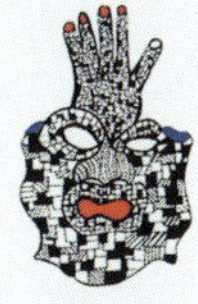

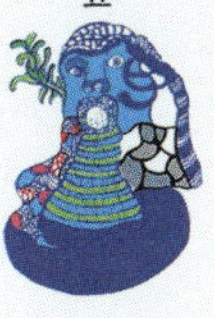

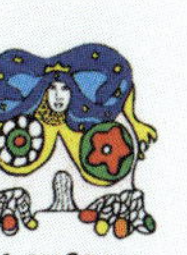

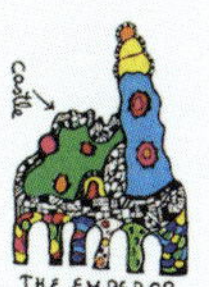

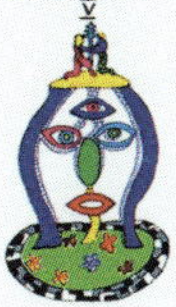

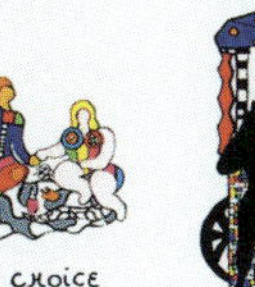

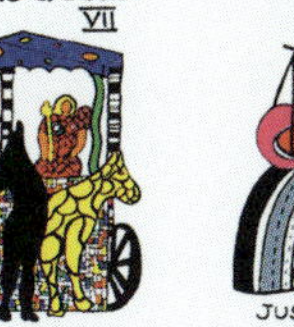

VIII
JUSTICE

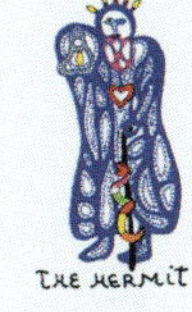

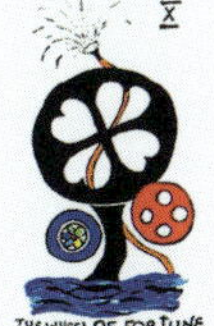

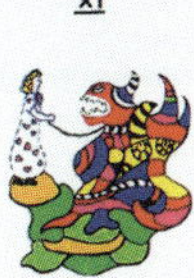

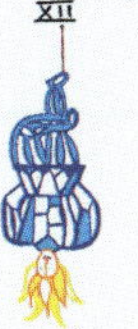

XIII
DEATH

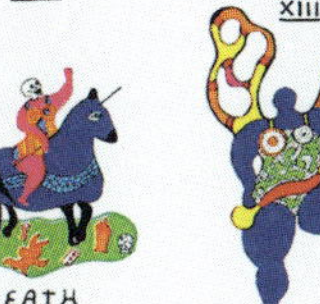

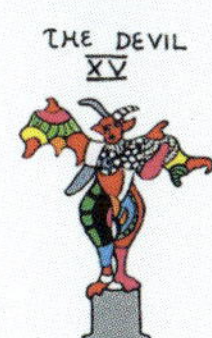

XVI
THE TOWER OF BABEL

XVII
THE STAR

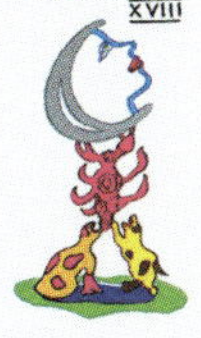

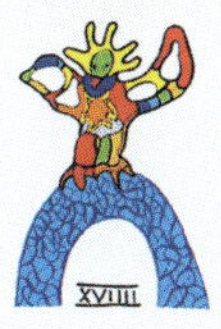

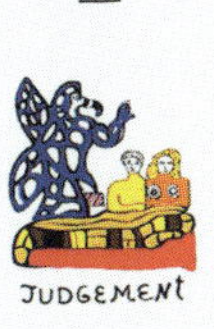

XXI
THE WORLD

Imprimé
© 2002
et
Productions

Niki de Saint Phalle

Tarot Cards 2000 screen print 80 × 60 cm

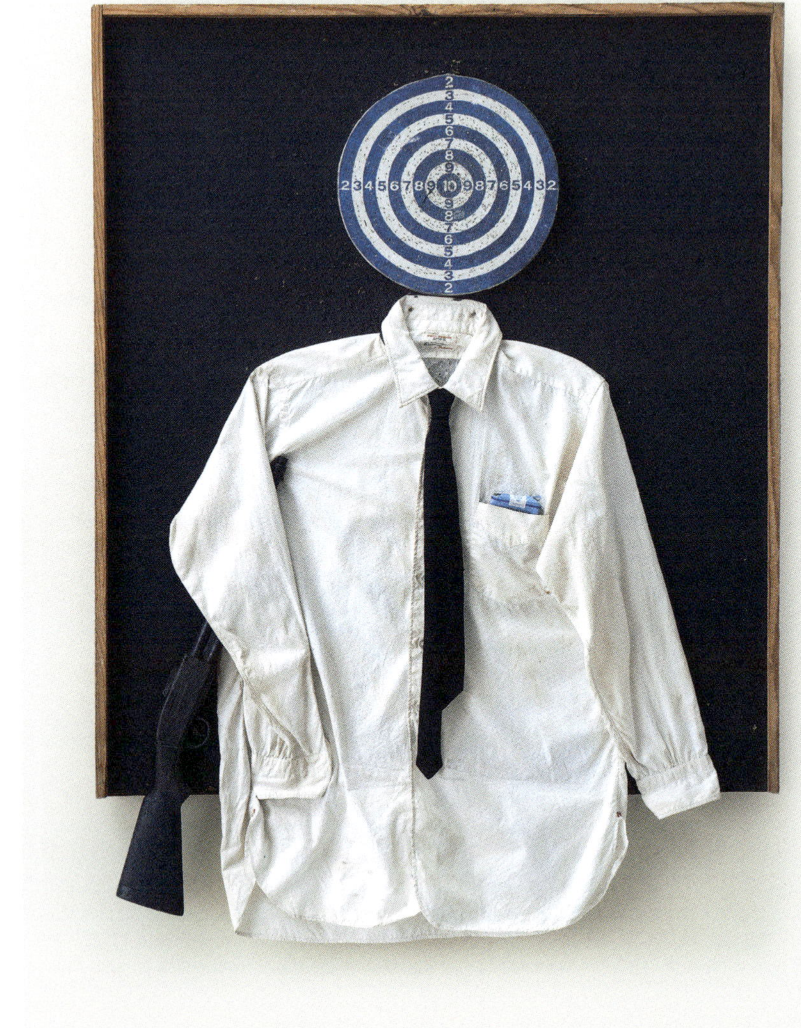

Martyr nécessaire / Saint Sébastien / Portrait de mon amour / Portrait of Myself
(Necessary Martyr / Saint Sebastian / Portrait of My Lover / Portrait of Myself) 1961 123 × 91 × 14 cm

U→ Uncanny

In his essay on the uncanny, Sigmund Freud outlined two facets of this quality and its effect.[38] In his view phenomena seem uncanny to us if we cannot say precisely whether they are alive or dead. And we experience the formerly familiar as uncanny when we have repressed it, but it appears again suddenly and unexpectedly. Niki de Saint Phalle took up both facets of the uncanny and lent them an aesthetic form.

The first variant is found in her *Shooting Paintings*, →Shooting in which she sometimes chose human figures as the targets for the actions. She and the audience shot darts at *Portrait of My Lover* (1961), which consisted of a white man's shirt with a tie and a dart as head. Or she fired rifles at plaster replicas, for example, of the *Venus de Milo* (1962), of an ancient male torso, or a figure of Christ on her "altars" (1962), causing their "life blood" to stream out of bags of paint behind the plaster. The processual quality of her actions, in which the fluids seemed to pour out of the wounds of art bodies of their own accord, could cause those present to be uncertain for a moment whether the statues did not in fact conceal a spark of life. That often produced a much greater thrill than the usurpation of a phallic instrument of killing by a woman or female artist. Niki de Saint Phalle herself speaks of rapture that seizes her when confronted with her power to create works that move along the dividing line between destruction and creation, killing and bringing to life: "I imagined the painting bleeding—wounded; the way people can be wounded. For me, the painting became a person with feelings and sensations."[39] And: "The painting is dead. I have killed the painting. It is reborn."[40]

That was further heightened when Niki de Saint Phalle turned to what she had herself repressed. As a precursor to the #MeToo activists, she tried in her art to address having been sexually abused by her father in order to make it public. Again and again, she made menacing and violent masculinity and sexuality the subject of her aesthetic exorcism. In both of her films,→Film she made use of surrealistic fantasies of violence and fairy-tale-like scenarios of taming in order to assimilate these experiences.
In her *Shooting Paintings*, destroying a variety of images

of masculinity was a radical, comprehensive liberation: "I shot because it was fun and made me feel good," she writes. "I shot against DADDY, against All Men, small men, Tall Men, Big Men, Fat Men, My Brother, society, the church, the convent, school, my family, my mother, ALL MEN, DADDY, Myself, Men."[41] By means of repetition, she gave her list the form of an evocative litany, while the capitalization gave her worst enemies the weight of a supra-individual authority. Saint Phalle once again proved to be a politically active artist who saw her personal experience as being anchored in structural inequities.

The uncanny also included "Myself," which appears in the litany almost casually and surprisingly. The artist experienced violence against her in two ways: as sexual and structural violence against her and as her own desire and will to employ violence.[42] Elsewhere she formulated this profound uncertainty as a question for Jean Tinguely → Jean Tinguely and herself: "Who is the monster, you or me?"[43] In her *Shooting Paintings*, Niki de Saint Phalle worked through for the first time the anguish caused by the uncanny self. It was a personal liberation: "By shooting at my own violence, I no longer had to carry it inside of me like a burden."[44]

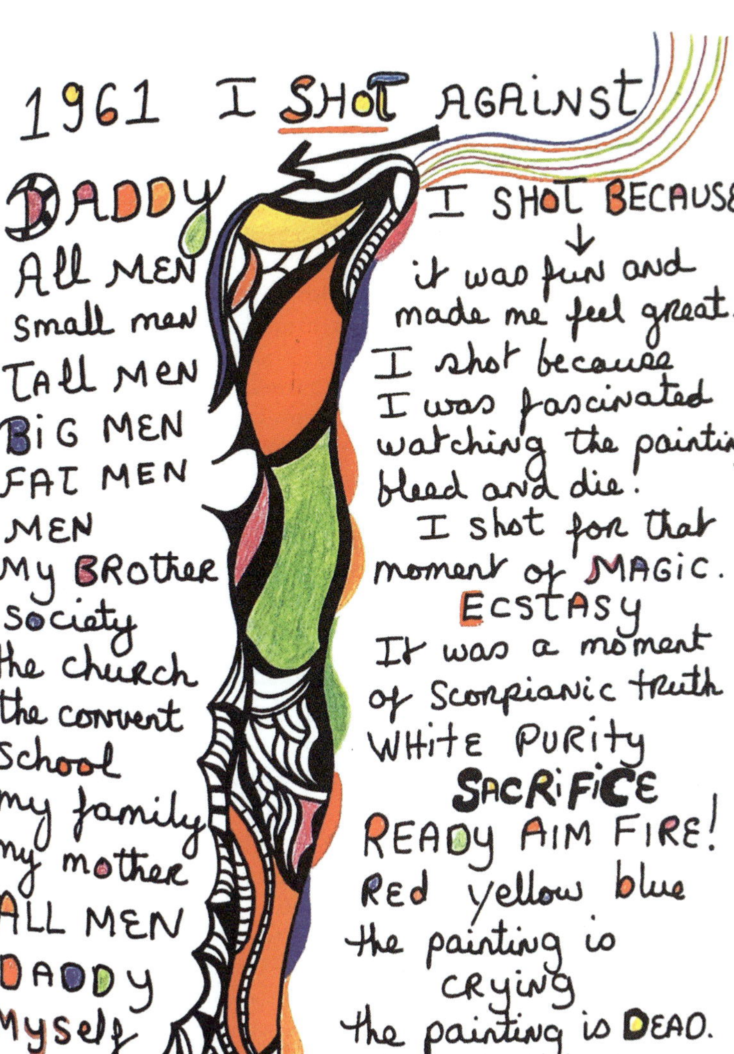

I Shot against Daddy published 1987

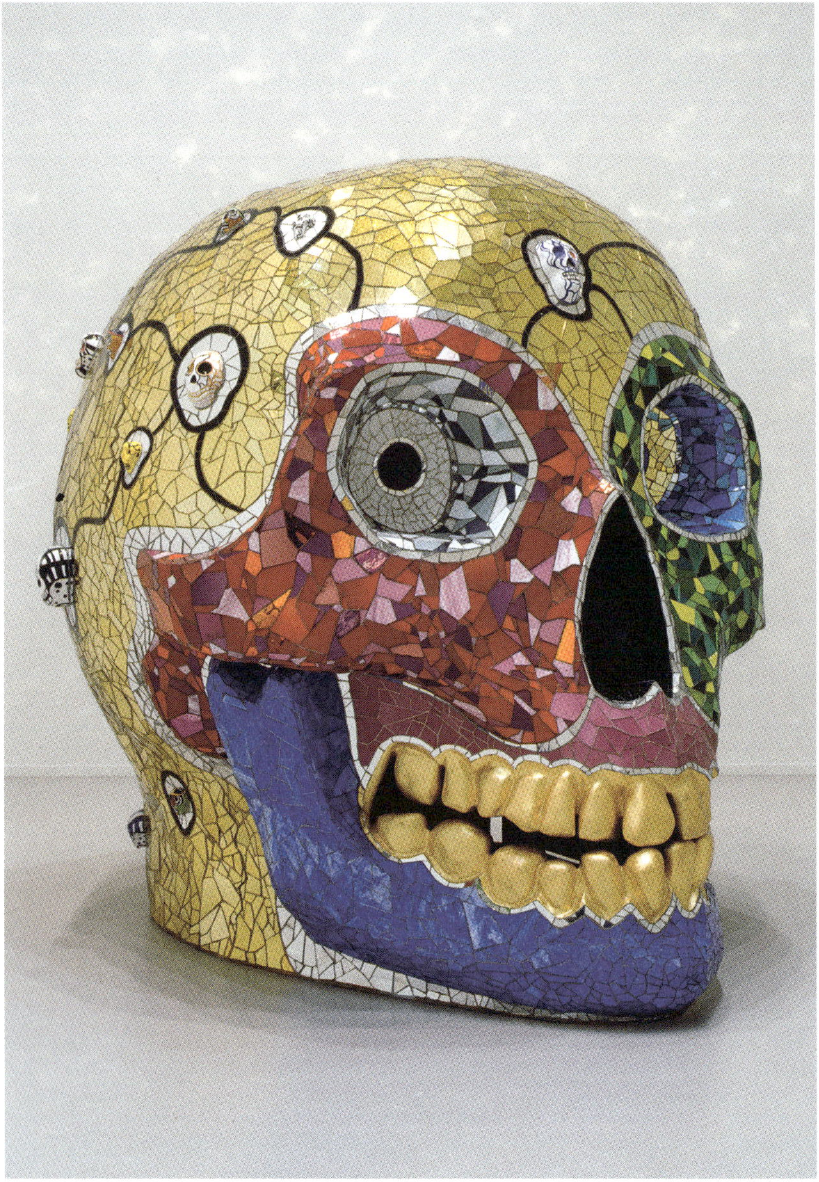

Skull, Meditation Room **1990**

V→ Vanitas

Immediately after the death of Jean Tinguely,→Jean Tinguely Niki de Saint Phalle came across a Baroque *vanitas* painting in Seville that impressed her and to which she was especially receptive in that situation: "I came into contact with 'Vanitas paintings' of the 17th century. These somber fascinating images of death (not devoid of black humor) stuck in my mind and suited my mood and I began drawing a series of *Vanitas tableaux éclatés*. I plunged into this world."[45]

Vanitas is generally equated with vanity. The Old Testament term it translates, *hebel*, means "vapor," and it is only its Latin translation that added the moral meaning of the trivial and vain. In the early modern period, the spectrum of the word's meanings expanded to include "appearance, futility, the dream, lack of utility and sense, . . . but also the void, the ephemeral, the transitory, and the transient."[46]

Niki de Saint Phalle had no interest at all in a lament about the vanishing of life but instead made the vanitas, in the sense of the fleeting and of the metamorphosis, a central driving force behind her art. She employed the traditional emblems →Emblem of the skull for transience, the arcane symbols of the tarot,→Tarot and the polymorphous fertility symbols of the tree of serpents →Polymorphy as figures of transformation.

One immanently artistic form of expression of the vanitas for her is the theme of passing time. This could occur as a sudden turn from one opposite to the other—for example, from the stasis and hermeticism of her whitewashed plaster reliefs to the bursting, streaming surface of the *Shooting Paintings* →Shooting —but also from the round corporeality to the weightlessness of the dancing *Nanas*. →Nana, →Kinetics It could, however, also happen in the slow movements of the figures of her waterworks →Water Fountain or in Tinguely's *Wheel of Fortune*, which turns at a leisurely pace in a pool in the *Tarot Garden*. →p. 30 Saint Phalle always produced a clearly perceptible "proper time" of the works and their aesthetics that is communicated to the viewers not only visually, but also physically as a personal experience.

In her modern instrumentalization of the vanitas, the aspect of transition was an important one for Saint

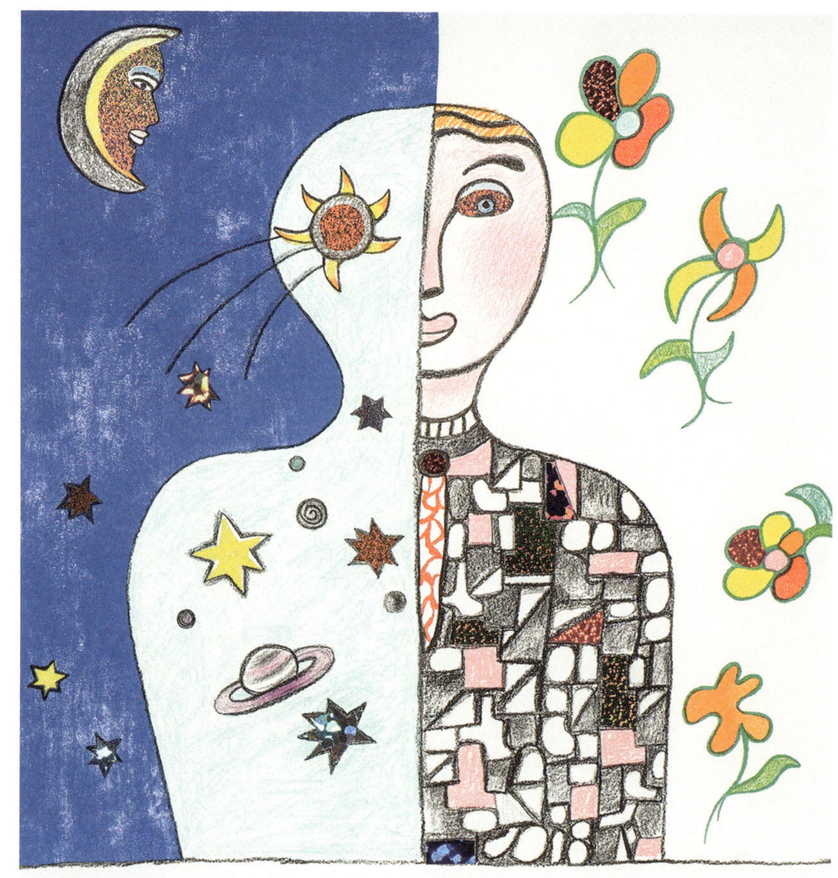

La mort n'existe pas / Life Is Eternal 2001 screen print 61.6 × 48 cm

Phalle. As in the Baroque, behind it lay a grappling with the most existential of all transitions: the passage to death. The artist did not, however, situate that exclusively at the end of life; she also impregnated the entry into life with it. For example, her assemblages of mothers giving birth, with their torn-up bodies, offer a look at post-mortem decay. The existential knowledge of having been born for death thus marks her entire oeuvre, but not in the way one might expect. Saint Phalle did not react with melancholy or repression, but rather took up the vanitas aspect of the memento mori in a way to point out the preciousness of every moment of life. She derived her colorful art that embraced humanity and the multifariousness of the world →Xenophilia, →Polymorphy not from naivete →Regression but rather from an awareness that all material things are finite.

Just as death is already inherent in the beginning of life, Niki de Saint Phalle conversely interpreted death as the moment that produces the new: a cyclical time of birth and death. Her drawing *La mort n'existe pas* (Death Does Not Exist), which shows a half-figure divided vertically, exemplifies this view. On the right side is a young man with a rosy face, eyes opened expectantly, in a colorfully patterned shirt, surrounded by bright flowers; on the left side is just his silhouette as a pure linear form in which planets and stars romp about in the blue night sky. That is not its negation but its reinterpretation. "Death Does Not Exist" means: "There is no absolute end."

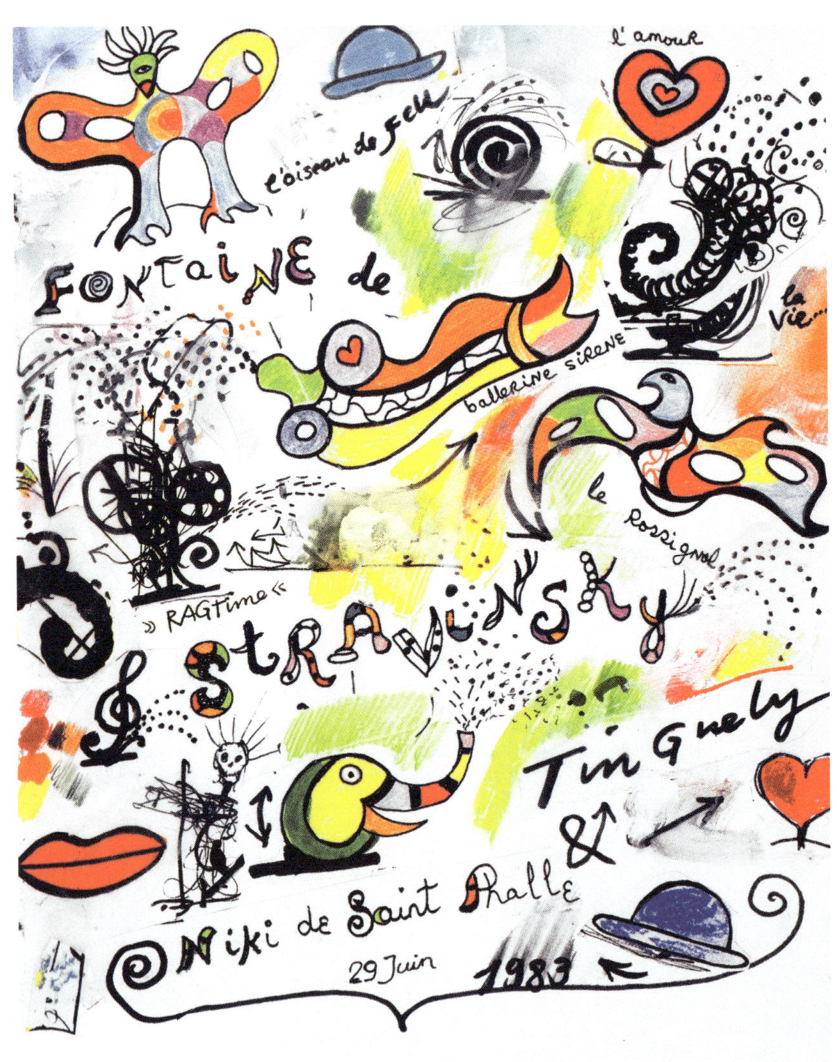
l'oiseau de feu
l'amour
Fontaine de
ballerine sirene
la vie....
le Rossignol
» RAGTime «
Stravinsky
Tinguely
&
Niki de Saint Phalle
29 Juin
1983

W→ Water Fountain

In 1977, a commission was being negotiated that would lead to one of the most popular works of Niki de Saint Phalle's collaboration with Jean Tinguely:→ Jean Tinguely the Stravinsky Fountain in Paris. Pierre Boulez, the director of the Institut de Recherche et de Coordination Acoustique/Musique in Paris, wanted to have a fountain built as an homage to that composer on the square named after him located between the newly built Centre Pompidou, the Gothic Church of Saint-Merri, the institute, and a row of old Parisian buildings. Boulez was enthusiastic about the *Fastnachtsbrunnen* (Carnival Fountain) that Jean Tinguely had created in Basel between 1975 and 1977, where ten sculptures and relics from a demolished theater in a pool shoveled, sprayed, rotated, and created waves to provide a humorous battle on water. Tinguely had accepted the offer on the condition that Saint Phalle and her colorful sculptures would be part of it and signed the contract in September 1982. Because the two had been working for two years preparing for the project with drawings and mock-ups, the fountain could be presented to the public just half a year later, on March 16, 1983. "Bringing life into this wasteland, that already meant something, but life suited to the man after whom it was named, that sounded almost utopian! Well—sometimes such ambitions can be satisfied, and utopia can become reality." That is how Boulez described the successful realization of his dream.[47]

In the Stravinsky Fountain, the sculptures of Niki de Saint Phalle and Jean Tinguely met "on water" for the first time. The outline of the pool was adapted to the rectangular ground plan of the square and confines the fluid element within the frame of a horizontal tableau consisting of a reflecting flat surface. The figures and assemblages, by contrast, set it in motion.→ Kinetics They spray water out of many openings in the form of fans, rays, and burbling, playing together like the instruments of an orchestra. The light reflected on the water's surface and refracted in its spray plays the second part of this musical piece for water. And the rotating and bending figures tap out its rhythm. The fountain is like a piece of music whose melody is water.

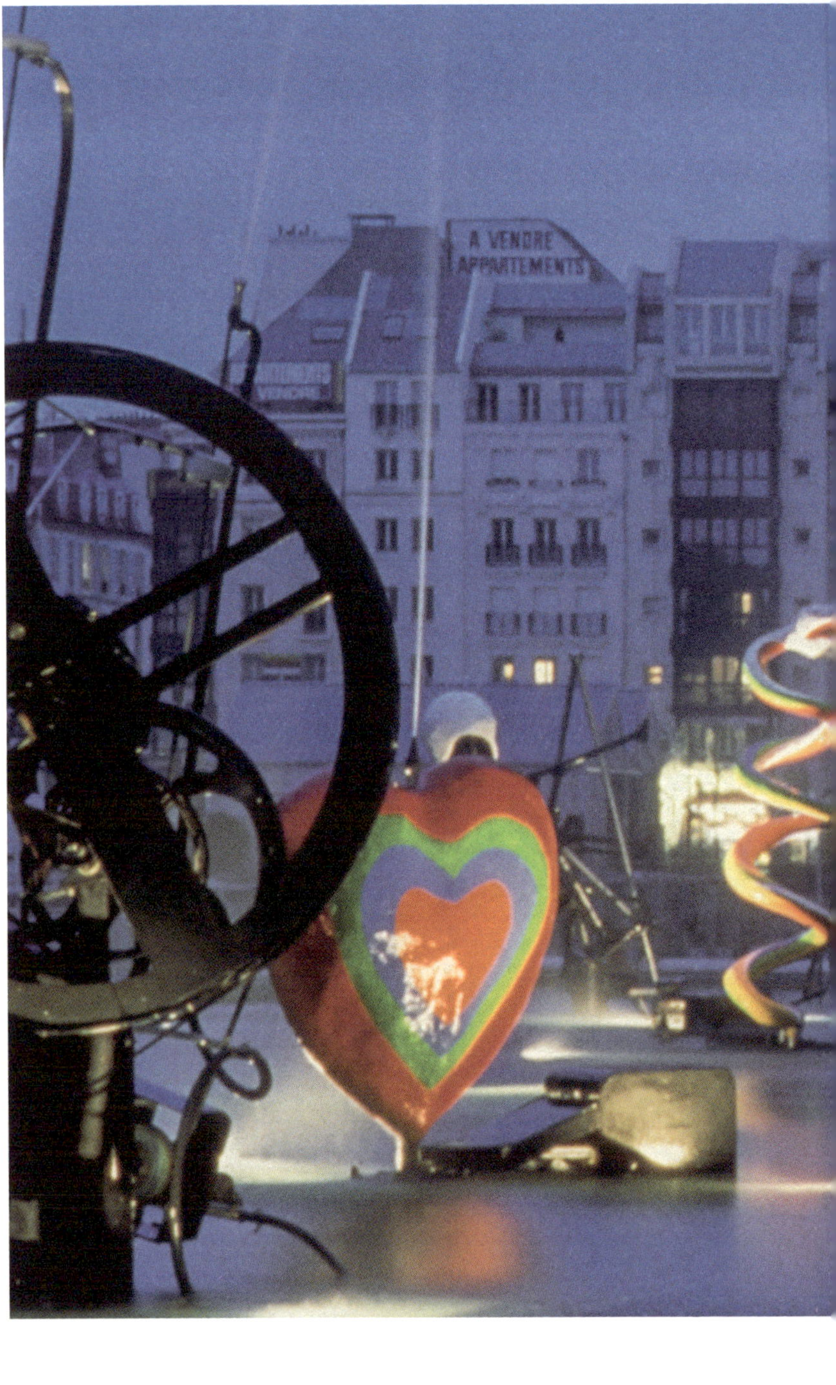

The Stravinsky Fountain in front of the Centre Pompidou 1983

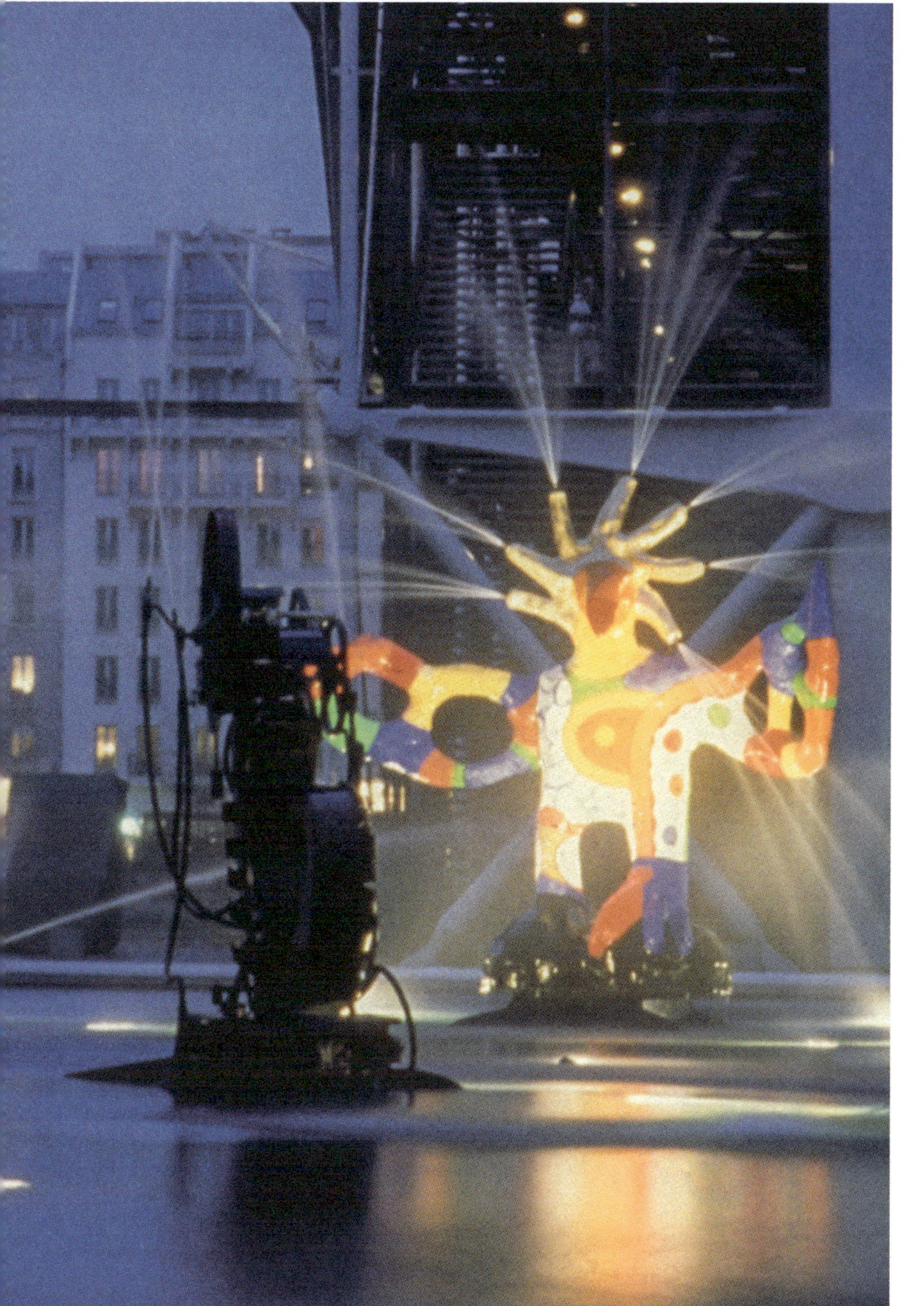

A large clef sets the tone for the ensemble, but none of the figures dance to its tune. Niki de Saint Phalle's giant kissing mouth, heart, and clown's hat turn now to the other sculptures, now to the public. Her *Oiseau de feu* (Firebird) and *Rossignol* (Nightingale) and Tinguely's *Renard* (Fox) and *Ragtime* refer directly to Stravinsky's fairy-tale-like ballet compositions and take up the motif of the dance.

In the Stravinsky Fountain, water is an aesthetic raw material of the composition.[48] Its fluidity and its refraction of light diminish the contrast between Tinguely's black-painted, mechanoid constructions and Saint Phalle's colorful, ample sculptures. Water causes all the figures to float on its surface, despite their differences in mass, and connects them to one another not in a battle of antitheses but in a childlike, erotic play of spraying and shrinking back, splashing and swimming. The mermaid bathes calmly in the water, while the firebird sprays an entire wreath of water jets from his head as if it wanted to transform its *feu d'artifice* (fireworks) into an *eau d'artifice* (artistic waterworks).

Niki de Saint Phalle and Jean Tinguely took up the idea of fountains from the garden traditions of many cultures, which were intended to refresh and entertain visitors. At the same time, they democratized tradition by making these benefits accessible to an urban audience. The Stravinsky Fountain is an especially popular attraction in the summer for that reason. Visitors approach it from the four corners of the Place Stravinsky and do not have an overview of the ensemble initially. Only by walking around the fountain do we discover ever-new perspectives on the changing configuration.[49] Through this circling movement, we join the dance in Saint Phalle and Tinguely's fountain.[50]

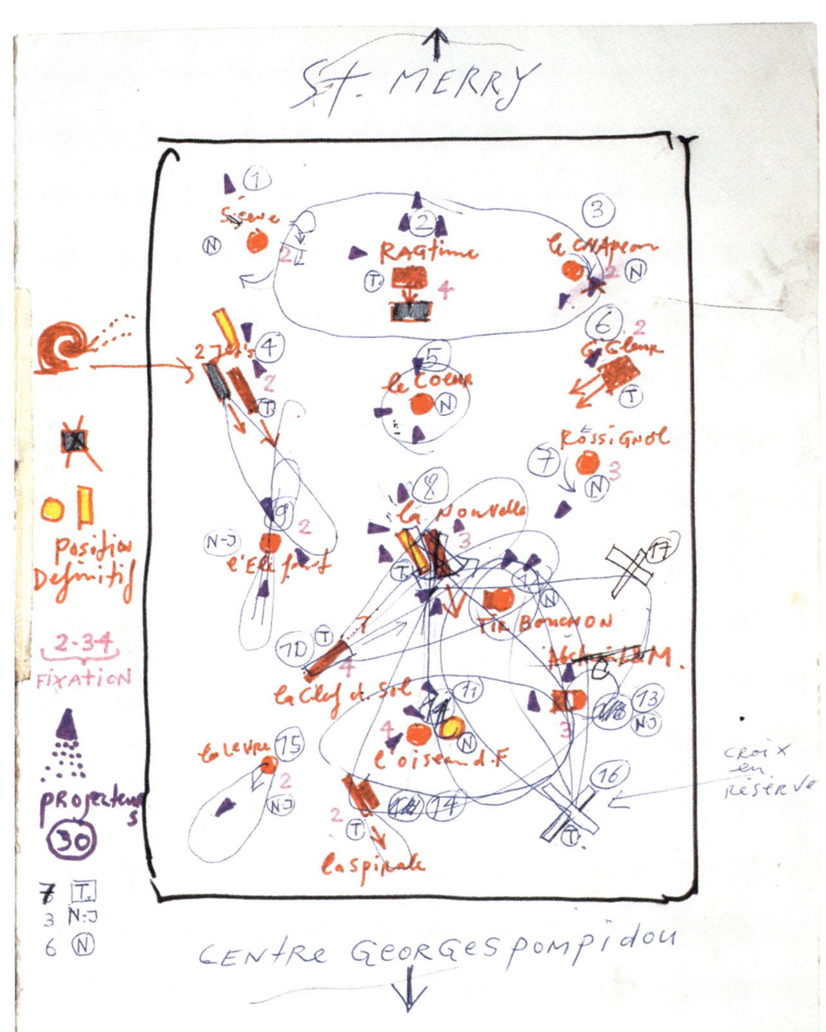

Jean Tinguely Site sketches for the (constantly changing) placement of the sculptures in the fountain

x→ Xenophilia

Niki de Saint Phalle was partial to the foreign all her life. That may have been a result of her self-assessment: "I am a special case. An Outsider," she writes.[51] This stranger can be people of another skin color, another gender, another species, or other art forms. The artist's xenophilia, or love of the foreign, was not limited to being open to and tolerant of various facets of the unknown, unusual, or different; rather, she truly adopted them. The artist saw herself as a permeable person who established no fixed boundaries between herself and the other. For example, when she encountered unfamiliar cultures and landscapes in California, these impressions and influences entered her as if by osmosis. "In Southern California I became a sponge," she writes, " permeable to the sea, mystery, immensity of nature, trees, air, animals, earth, sand, people."[52] That was also true of non-Western art, which by her own account she had virtually swallowed whole. Recognizing her inspiration cultures, she writes with self-ironic distance: "I see myself as a devouring mother who has devoured all sorts of varied influences from Giotto, early Sienese paintings, Douanier Rousseau, Mexican and Indian temples, to Bosch and Arcimboldo, to Picasso, and they have been eaten and absorbed and the child that is born from that feast is invariably a Niki."[53] Distinguishing herself from the Western ideal of the artist-genius, Saint Phalle saw herself as an artist who became creative not through divine inspiration but through receptivity to all the phenomena that surrounded her.

In gender relationships, conversely, Niki de Saint Phalle deliberately perceived her own position as an experience of foreignness, with which she had been stamped as an inferior female by a male-oriented social structure. Taking up attributes of masculinity such as the rifle →Shooting and equating herself with the monster as a symbol of male power →Uncanny were therefore actions of usurpation and adaption that symbolically placed both sexes on eye level. The same is true of Saint Phalle's love of people from other cultures and of other skin color. In words and images, she repeatedly celebrated Black men and women and created a monument of greatness and strength for them with her *Queen Califia*.→Queen Califia "Black is different," she writes. “I have made many black figures in my work. Black Venus, black Madonna, black men, black Nanas. It has always been an important color for me.”[54] As a gesture of empowerment, such aesthetic and rhetorical statements aim politically to create solidarity and overcome discrimination.

In terms of her own family history, Saint Phalle also welcomed the broadening of her genealogy with people of other skin color and origin. She was enthusiastic about her great-grandson Djamal, who was of mixed heritage, and integrated his multiethnicity into her own personality: “Black is also me with my great grandson Djamal. This is new and I like it. Djamal is French, American, Vietnamese, Greek, Belgian, Irish, English, African, Scottish, Russian, Italian, Jewish, Cuban = American. Black is also me now.”[55] With a refrain repeated as if in a gospel song, “I too am black,” the artist actively defined herself as part of an America that once derived its positive identity from the fact that it was a melting pot of all the cultures of the world—an idea that is at risk of getting lost today in separatist identity politics. Niki de Saint Phalle’s xenophilia as emphatic appreciation aimed to democratize society by demonstratively rejecting racist distinctions.

Black Is Different 1994 screen print 80 × 120 cm

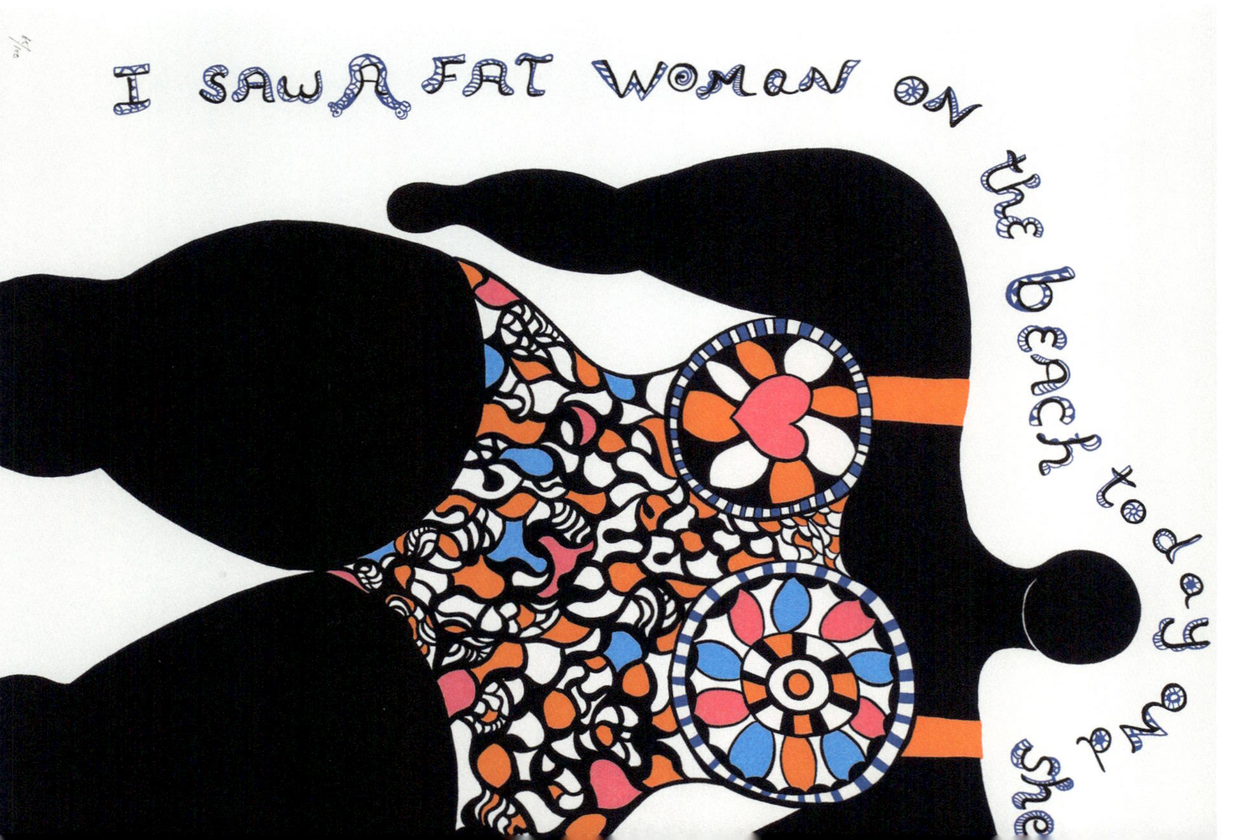

ear Diary,

EMINDED ME OF A GREAT PAGAN GODDESS

BLACK is DIFFERENT.

I have made MANY
BLACK FIGURES
in my WORK.
BLACK VENUS, BLACK MADONNA,
BLACK MEN, BLACK NANAS.
It has always been an important
color for me.
Today, walking on the beach
I watched a small black child
5 or 6 years old playing with his father.
He was SO CUTE. It was
a REVELATION.
Black is ALSO ME NOW
with my great grandson Djamal. This is NEW
and I like it.
Djamal is: FRENCH, American Vietnamese,
Greek, Belgian, Irish, English, African,
Scottish, Russian, Italian, Jewish, Cuban.
= AMERICAN
Black is also me Now. Niki St. Phalle

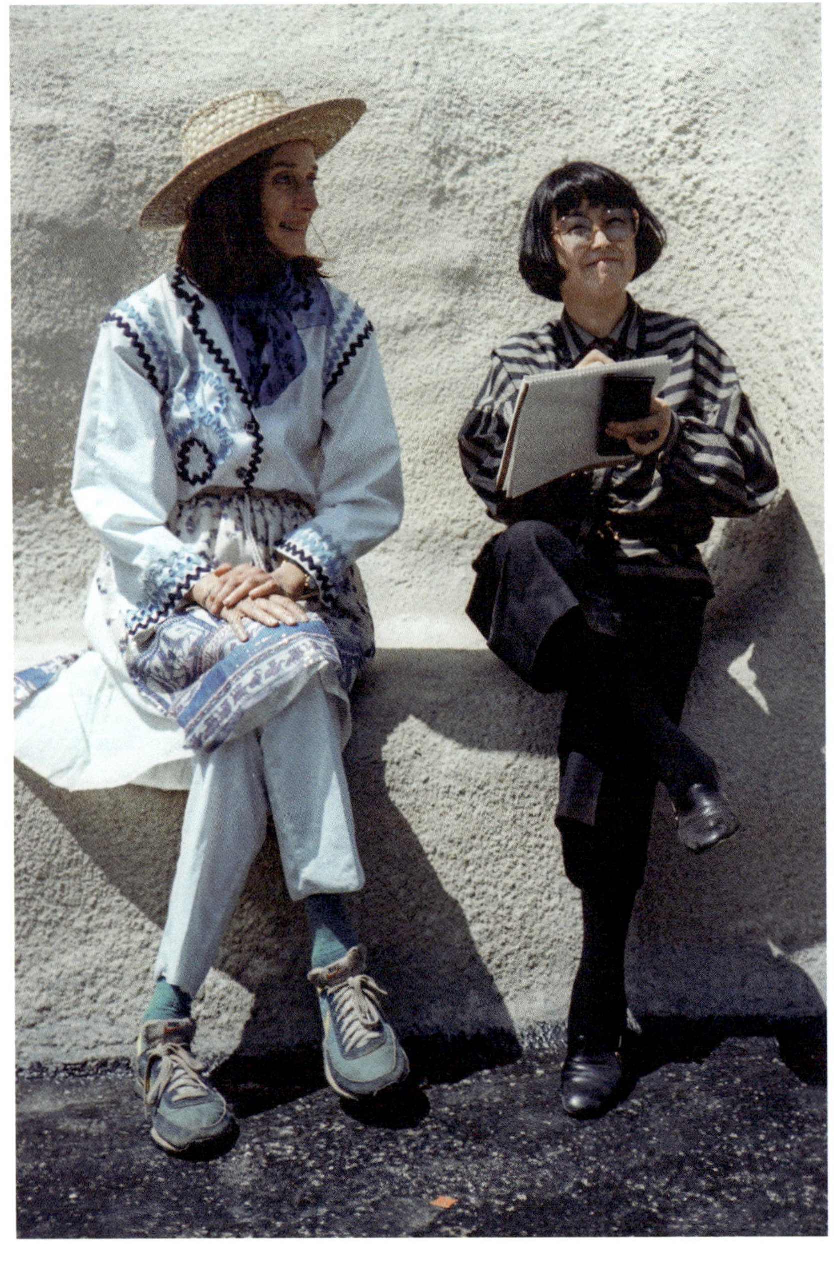

Yoko Shizue Masuda visiting Niki de Saint Phalle, on the roof terrace of *The Empress* where Niki lives and works in the Tarot Garden May 1985

Y→ Yoko Shizue Masuda

At the height of summer in 1980, there was a consequential encounter in Tokyo. The businesswoman Shizue Masuda saw a print by Niki de Saint Phalle for the first time: the fictive *Letter to My Lover*,[56] decorated with colorful emblems.→Emblem She was so fascinated by its visual language that she tried to learn as much about the artist as she could and bought all of the works without asking the price. That same year she opened a gallery space dedicated exclusively to the artist's works in her company's building in the Ueno district: Space Niki. Shizue Masuda's passion for collecting focused on Saint Phalle, and her empathetic connoisseurship of her oeuvre soon led to a lifelong friendship. They met in Paris as early as 1981. From then on, they remained in contact across continents. More than three hundred letters from Niki de Saint Phalle, most of them illustrated, testify to this.

Both women were connected across their priviledged but different cultures by the fact that they were literally self-made women. It is no coincidence that their names, Niki and Yoko, seem to echo each other,[57] since they had named themselves. The artist had formed the androgynous abbreviation Niki from her baptismal name Catherine Marie-Agnès. For her part, Yoko Shizue Masuda realized that Niki de Saint Phalle had difficulty pronouncing her name.[58] She therefore chose the short name Yoko for her new friend, with two kanji characters, the first of which means "sun" or "ocean," and the second "child"—a clear reference to the artist's emblems →Emblem and visual language.→Regression

Yoko Shizue Masuda made Niki's art world her own. Or vice versa: she was, as she wrote, "swallowed by a monster called Niki."[59] She plunged into the artist's mythology and added to it ideas from Japanese culture and East Asian religions. And she became the most important Japanese mediator of Saint Phalle's art. To house the private collection of 260 works from all phases of the artist's career that she put together over the years, she built her own museum. In the city of Nasu in Tochigi Prefecture, she had a series of airy pavilions built in which hundreds of works, from *Shooting Paintings* by way of large sculptures to drawings, were on permanent exhibit. The prizewinning building is embedded in a garden whose character changes with every season, thus taking into account the ideal of transformation in Niki de Saint Phalle's art. In parallel with the *Tarot Garden* → Tarot, → Garden in Tuscany, the Niki Museum opened in 1994 as a kindred pendant to the artist's largest Gesamtkunstwerk.[60]

Four years after the museum's opening, Niki de Saint Phalle visited Japan for the first time and was enthusiastic about the building, the park, and the presentation of the collection. She was just as impressed by Japanese ritual art in the temples and the Japanese art of drawing with its abbreviations, to which she felt a spiritual and aesthetic relationship. In a bow to Japanese culture, Saint Phalle then began to create figures that can be traced back to her encounter with Japan: an imposing Buddha sculpture in the Niki Museum in Nasu closed the circle of transcultural encounter embodied in the friendship of the two women.

Yoko Shizue Masuda and Niki de Saint Phalle, the Japanese collector and the Franco-American artist, defined their decades-long friendship as fateful and made comparable experiences as women and the desire to unfold feminine creativity and strength the transnational link of their joint project. They were convinced that they had met in a previous life, the one as a witch and the other as her judge. They imagined they would meet in their next life in other roles: Yoko Shizue Masuda as an internationally celebrated singer and Niki de Saint Phalle as her devoted groupie. They both enjoyed laughing together.[61]

Yoko Shizue Masuda passed away on January 29, 2009. Two years later, the museum closed. But her collection lives on in numerous exhibitions.

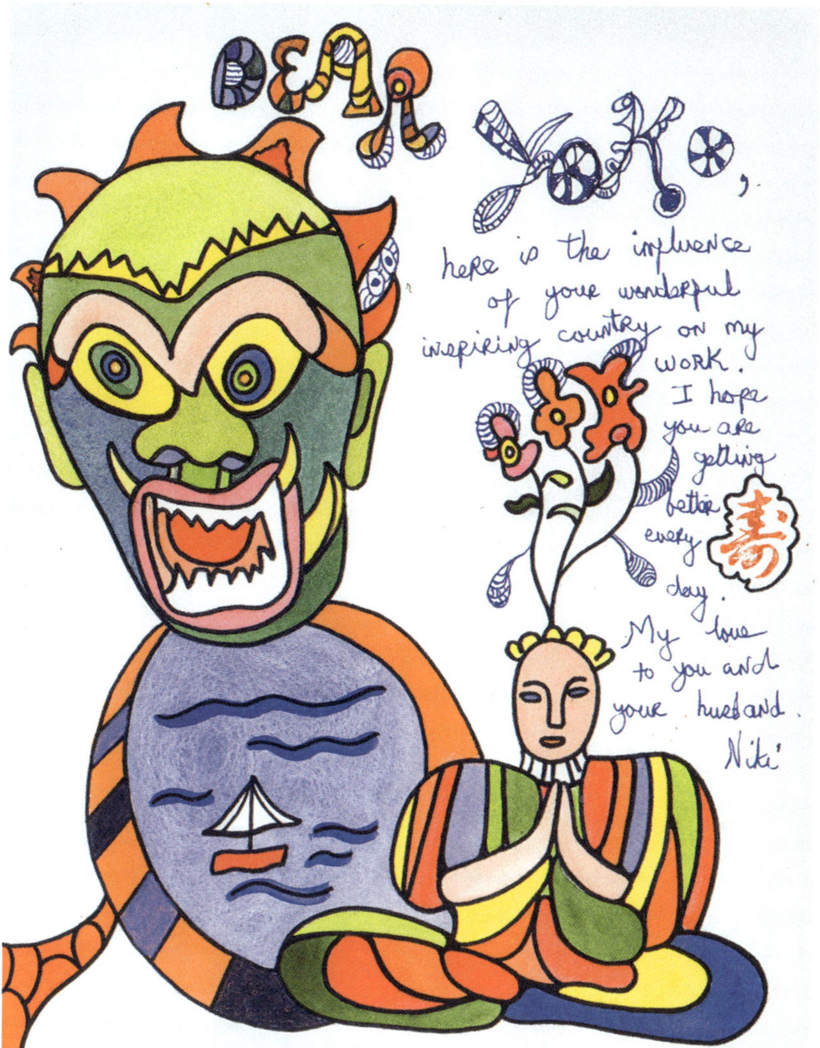

DEAR YOKO,

here is the influence
of your wonderful
inspiring country on my
WORK.
I hope
you are
getting
better
every
day.
My love
to you and
your husband.
Niki

寿

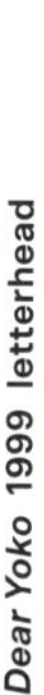

Dear Yoko 1999 letterhead

Z→ Zurich's Angel

In 1997, Niki de Saint Phalle was commissioned by the Swiss railway company: she was to create a large sculpture for the main hall of Zurich's central train station. It was the era of her *Tarot Garden*,→Tarot, →Garden and so she replicated one of its figures and flew it to Zurich from the earthly paradise of Tuscany. It is the female guardian angel that in the tarot stands for prudence and temperance (*temperantia*).

In the Tuscan sculpture park, *Temperance* is a dark-blue *Nana* with golden, perforated wings and breasts decorated with a heart and a flower, dancing on the dome of a chapel. The vault of the latter repeats the curves of her bust, and the surface of mirror shards that reflect their surroundings take up the transparency of her wings. The figure is pouring a red fluid from one pitcher to another. As the embodiment of balance between extremes, the female angel protects against destruction and regulates the flow of vital energy. That also makes her the guarantor that the connection between the past and the future will remain unbroken.

The chapel houses a grotto that is also completely decorated with mirror mosaics. Inside, however, it does not reflect the sky and trees but rather candlelight. A second guardian figure is found on the altar: a black Madonna and Child, under whose guardianship the votive images of the artist's friends who were ill or had already died.[62] As with the monumental sculpture *Hon*,→Hon the architecture and the female body fuse and become the primal image of a sacred protective shell. The angel from the Major Arcana of the tarot and the Christian Mother of God mark the inside and outside as female zones of a syncretic protective power. The architectural reference here is not the cathedral but the intimate chapel that invites introspection.

The train stations of the industrial age were seen as secular cathedrals of modernity. With their enormous domes, they absorbed the crowds of travelers and released them again on their numerous rails leading in all directions of the compass. Their immense roofs of glass and steel protected the travelers from the weather. The ticket counters and display boards in their halls offered them orientation,

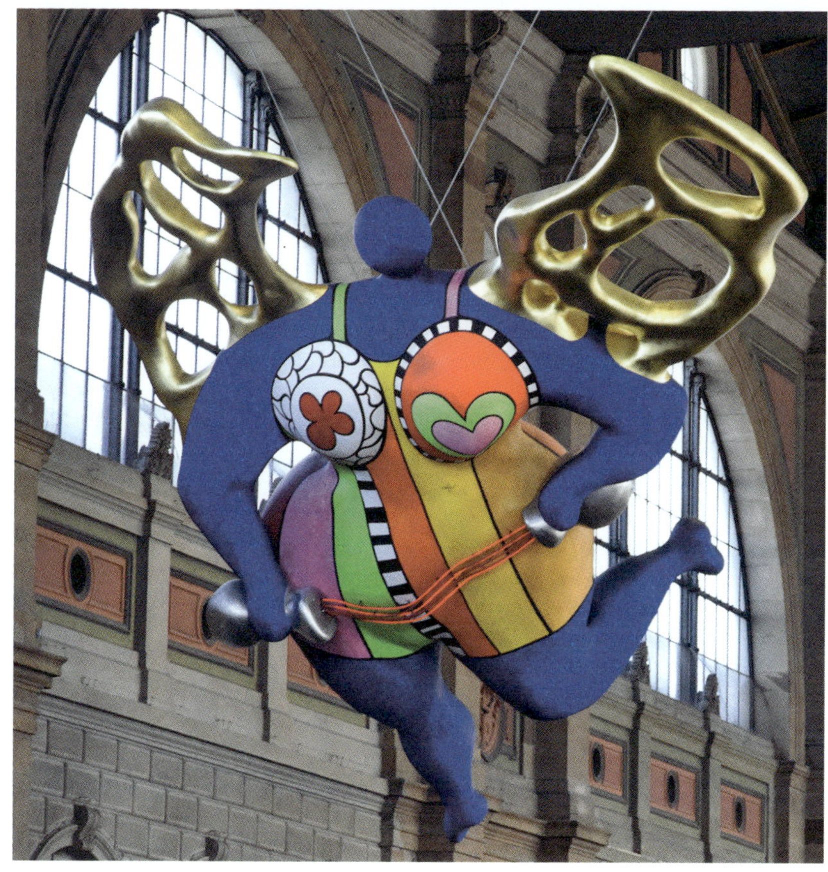

L'ange protecteur (Guardian Angel) 1997

and the restaurants and shops fed them. Like Niki de Saint Phalle's devouring and birthing mothers,[→Mothers] nineteenth-century train stations had become dense, ambiguous metaphors.

The scale and placement of the *L'ange protecteur* (guardian angel)[→p. 104] in Zurich take up the practical and ideal functions of the train station and translate them into a symbolic sculpture. Like the Madonna icon in the chapel of the *Tarot Garden*, it is placed in the interior of a building. It is elevated, not enthroned like a devotional sculpture on an altar but rather floating in the airy realm of the gable roof. At ten meters tall, the angel sculpture also adopts the scale of this monumental building. The main hall provides it with enough room for its dancing high flight. The dress has subtle features. A black-and-white band circles the red breast with its heart, and a second one leads longitudinally from the other breast to the hem of the dress. The flow of life is led from one silver jug to another in the form of parallel red threads. The rails and platforms are echoed in these linear patterns. Saint Phalle takes up the significance and emblem of *Temperance* as the embodiments of a balanced life and translates it into the guardian angel of modern train travel for its architectural context in Zurich.

Its movement[→Kinetics] also makes Niki de Saint Phalle's angel in Zurich an embodiment of the pleasure of travel. Its striving for the heights accompanies the horizontal stream of people through the main hall to the platforms of this terminus. It symbolically lends them wings as they set out into the wide world and takes them under its wings again when they return. As a relative of the *Temperance*, the guardian angel shows that departure and homecoming condition each other and should be kept in balance. It welcomes the travelers both when they depart and when they arrive.

The text was written in 2022.

1 ACT UP stands for "AIDS Coalition to Unleash Power." It is a group of activists founded in New York in 1987 that works internationally on medical education and to end political discrimination against those infected with HIV.
2 The medieval Frau Welt sculpture is a symbol of earthly pleasures that shows a beautiful young woman who is being eaten by worms in the back. It is a moralizing allegory of the transience of all happiness.
3 Quoted in Rudick 2022, p. 145.
4 Quoted in ibid., pp. 98–99.
5 Quoted in ibid., p. 143.
6 Saint Phalle 1999, p. 6.
7 Ibid., pp. 6–7.
8 Quoted in Rudick 2022, p. 220.
9 See "Lettre à Marcella Caracciolo," in Paris 1993, p. 174.
10 The Hypnerotomachia Poliphili, as a combination of a description of a garden à l'antiqua and a romance, became the model for many later garden designs.
11 See Larry Rivers, in Basel 2020, p. 155.
12 Letter from Niki de Saint Phalle to Clarice Rivers, "Dearest Clarice," autumn 1966. Quoted in Rudick 2022, pp. 89–90, esp. p. 89.
13 The film is *Luffar-Petter* (Peter the Tramp) of 1922, dir. Erik A. Petchler.
14 Letter from Niki de Saint Phalle to Clarice Rivers, "Dearest Clarice," autumn 1966. Quoted in Rudick 2022, p. 90.
15 Saint Phalle 2006, p. 85.
16 See Elsa Noël-Guesnon, "The Women of the Impasse Ronsin: Creation, Rebellion, and Independence," in Basel 2020, pp. 195–99, esp. p. 199; Marta Minujín, "Destruction of My Works in the Impasse Ronsin, Paris," trans. Marguerite Feitlowitz, in Inés Katzenstein, ed., *Listen, Here, Now! Argentine Art of the 1960s: Writings of the Avant-Garde* (New York, 2004), pp. 59–61.
17 See Lütgens 2000.
18 See Éléonore Duchêne, "Les Bonnie & Clyde de l'art contemporain," in Paris 2014, pp. 42–46.
19 Niki de Saint Phalle, "A Little of My Story with You Jean," in Rudick 2022, pp. 222–36, esp. p. 236.
20 Ibid., p. 139.
21 Ibid., p. 147.
22 See Saint Phalle 1972.
23 The book measures 16.5 × 14 cm. Its forty-eight illustrated pages are punched between cardboard covers and bound by coarse threads.
24 Kalliopi Minioudaki, "Démasquer et réimag(in)er le féminin: Les mères de Niki de Saint Phalle," in Paris and Bilbao 2015, pp. 164–72, esp. p. 172.
25 Ibid.
26 Niki de Saint Phalle encountered the Venus of Willendorf only after inventing her *Nanas*. But she saw an elective affinity between their ideals of the body: "When I made the *Nanas*, I did not know about the Venus of Willendorf, one of the first sculptures to be created in a matriarchal society. She represented the goddess of fertility and looks just like one of my *Nanas*. When I saw pictures of this Venus, I was fascinated. The unconscious dreams of people who lived more than thirty thousand years ago were identical to my own." Niki de Saint Phalle, quoted in Schulz-Hoffmann 2003, p. 14.
27 Émile Zola, *Nana* (New York, 1928), p. 34.
28 See Mikhail Bakhtin, *Rabelais and His World*, trans. Hélène Iswolsky (Bloomington, IN, 1984; orig. pub. 1965).
29 Dortmund 2016, p. 142.
30 See Lucia Pesapane, "Le Jardin des Tarots entre imaginaire symbolique et mythologies personels," in Paris/Bilbao 2015, pp. 260–66, esp. p. 266.
31 See ibid.
32 Mélanie Gourarier writes of the Tarot Garden: "Peut-être le jardin des Tarots est-il une sorte de retour en arrière, un voyage initiatique à l'envers, une régression de l'artiste vers le monde de l'enfance et de l'innocence? Niki de Saint Phalle nous invite alors à entrer dans son univers, au temps d l'enfance de l'humanité, dans ce paradis primordial situé ailleurs et hors du temps." (Perhaps the Tarot Garden is a kind of flashback, a journey of initiation in reverse, the artist's regressionto the childhood of humanity, to that primordial paradise that exists elsewhere and beyond time.) Gourarier 2010, p. 22.
33 Saint Phalle 1999, p. 69.
34 See Larry Rivers, in Basel 2020, p. 155.
35 See Pesapane 2015 (see note 30).
36 "I am the fool," Niki de Saint Phalle writes: "The fool hasn't done badly, never knowing where he is going, stumbling on his path, finding mysterious treasures and perilous adventures." Quoted in Rudick 2022, p. 132. See also Gourarier 2010, p. 72.
37 Niki de Saint Phalle, "Tarot Garden," in *Niki de Saint Phalle: My Art, My Dreams*, ed. Carla Schulz-Hoffmann (Munich, 2003), p. 136.
38 See Sigmund Freud, "The Uncanny" (1919), in *The Standard Edition of the Complete Psychological Works of Sigmund Freud*, ed. James Strachey (London, 1955), pp. 219–52.
39 Quoted in Rudick 2022, p. 79.
40 Ibid., p. 75.
41 Ibid.
42 See Wimmer 2006, pp. 78–109.
43 "Qui est le monstre toi ou moi?,"fictive letter from Niki de Saint Phalle to Jean Tinguely, 1990. Quoted in Rudick 2022, p. 64.
44 Quoted in Rudick 2022, p. 80.
45 Niki de Saint Phalle, "Death and Resurrection," in ibid., pp. 198–201, esp. p. 199.
46 Claudia Benthien and Victoria von Flemming, "Einleitung," in "Vanitas: Reflexionen über Vergänglichkeit in der Literatur, bildenden Kunst und theoretischen Diskursen der Gegenwart," special issue, *Paragrana: Internationale Zeitschrift für Anthropologie* 27, no. 2 (2018): 11–36, esp. 13.

47 Pierre Boulez, "Vorwort," in *Jean Tinguely and Niki de Saint Phalle, Strawinsky-Brunnen Paris* (Bern, 1983), pp. 8–9, esp. p. 8.
48 See Franz Meyer, "Wasseraktion und Wasserspektakel: Zur Vorgeschichte der Pariser 'Fontaine,'" in ibid., pp. 11–15, esp. p. 11.
49 See Stefanie Poley, "Die 'Fontaine Saint-Merri,'" in ibid., pp. 93–96.
50 "Je ne désire pas impressionner les gens, je désir jouer avec eux" (I do not want to impress people; I want to play with them), Tinguely said in a newspaper interview. Quoted in ibid., p. 96.
51 Niki de Saint Phalle, "Niki by Niki," in Rudick 2022, pp. 149–50, esp. p. 149.
52 Saint Phalle 2022 (see note 45).
53 Saint Phalle 2022 (see note 51).
54 Niki de Saint Phalle, "Dear Diary," in Rudick 2022, pp. 206–7, esp. p. 207.
55 Ibid.
56 See Yoko Masuda Shizue, "Fate & Passion: The Moment a Collector Tries to Be a Museum Founder," in *Niki de Saint Phalle* (Nagoya: Nagoya City Art Museum, 2006), p. 123.
57 See Camille Morineau, "Niki de Saint Phalle: Une artiste à deux faces," in ibid., pp. 214–16, esp. p. 215.
58 See Yoko Masuda Shizue, "Fate & Passion: The Moment a Collector Tries to Be a Museum Founder," in *Niki de Saint Phalle* (Nagoya: Nagoya City Art Museum, 2006), p. 122.
59 Yoko Shizue Masuda, "Her Friendship with Niki," Niki Museum Gallery, https://niki-museum.jp/contents/archives/gallery/niki_museum (accessed September 2, 2022).
60 Masuda reports that they shared their common interest in tarot cards already at their first meeting in Paris in June 1981. See Yoko Shizue Masuda, "My Nana Monster: Niki de Saint Phalle," in *Niki de Saint Phalle* (see note 56), pp. 222–28, esp. p. 227.
61 There is a postcard with a dedication by Niki de Saint Phalle: "For Shizue with many greetings thanks and good wishes and laughter from Niki June 1985," in *Niki de Saint Phalle* (see note 56), p. 111.
62 Niki de Saint Phalle set up the chapel as a votive gift for Jean Tinguely's recuperation after a heart operation. In addition, a portrait of Ricardo Menon, who was her assistant for many years and died in 1989, decorates the altar.

Photo Credits

P. 2: Photo: Robert Doisneau, © Robert Doisneau/GAMMA RAPHO
P. 4: Photo: Hans Hammarskiöld, © Hans Hammarskiöld Heritage
PP. 7–9: Details from *AIDS: You Can't Catch It Holding Hands*, 1986, published in Lapis Press, San Francisco
P. 15: bpk/Sprengel Museum Hannover, Gift Niki de Saint Phalle (2000)/Herling/Gwose/Werner
P. 16: Courtesy Galerie GP & N Vallois, Paris, Aurélien Mole
PP. 18/19, 20 (top), 75, 84, 96/97: bpk/Sprengel Museum Hannover/Michael Herling/Aline Gwose
P. 29: Michael Herling (Sprengel Museum Hannover)
P. 30: Photo: © Hans Jan Dürr
P. 35: David and Isabelle Lévy collection, Brussels
P. 37: Musée d'art et d'histoire Fribourg
PP. 40/41: © Christer Strömholm/Strömholm Estate
P. 43: Harry Shunk/János Kender (J. Paul Getty Trust. Getty Research Institute, Los Angeles)
P. 47: ETH-Bibliothek Zürich, Bildarchiv/Photo: Metzger, Jack/Com_L16-0320-0013-0003
P. 48: Photo: Niels Fabaek (Kunsten Museum of Modern Art, Aalborg)
PP. 50, 86: Sprengel Museum Hannover Gift Niki de Saint Phalle
P. 52: Moderna Museet/Stockholm
P. 54: © mumok – Museum moderner Kunst Stiftung Ludwig Wien, Leihgabe der Österreichischen Ludwig-Stiftung
PP. 56, 61: Sprengel Museum Hannover Gift Niki de Saint Phalle. Michael Herling (Sprengel Museum Hannover)
PP. 66/67: © Ed Schipul
P. 73: Peter Whitehead (Niki Charitable Art Foundation, Santee)
P. 79: Private collection Hannover, Ulrich Krempel
P. 80: Private collection Courtesy Galerie GP & N Vallois, Paris, André Morin
PP. 90/91: Photo: Leonardo Bezzola
P. 98: Photo: Masashi Kuroiwa, 1985

Bibliography (Selection)

Basel 2020
Impasse Ronsin: Murder, Love, and Art in the Heart of Paris. Edited by Giorgio Bloch, Adrian Dannatt, and Andres Perdey. Translated by Alexandra Cox and Jeremy Mercer. Exh. cat. Museum Jean Tinguely, Basel. Heidelberg, 2020.

Becker 1999
Becker, Monika. *Niki de Saint Phalle: Starke Weiblichkeit entfesseln*. 2nd ed. Munich, 1999.

Dortmund 2016
Ich bin eine Kämpferin: Frauenbilder der Niki de Saint Phalle/I'm a Fighter: Images of Women by Niki de Saint Phalle. Edited by Ulrich Krempel and Regina Selter. Translated by Michael Wolfson et al. Exh. cat. Museum am Ostwall, Dortmund. Berlin, 2016.

Gourarier 2010
Gourarier, Mélanie. *Niki de Saint Phalle: Le jardin des Tarots*. Arles, 2010.

Hannover 2001
La Fête: Die Schenkung Niki de Saint Phalle; Werke aus den Jahren, 1952–2001. Edited by Ulrich Krempel. Exh. cat. Sprengel Museum, Hannover. Hannover, 2001.

Lütgens 2000
Lütgens, Annelie. "L'esprit de Tinguely: Das Wunderbare besiegt das Nützliche." In *Jean Tinguely: L'esprit de Tinguely*. Exh. cat. Kunstmuseum Wolfsburg; Museum Jean Tinguely, Basel, pp. 19–23. Ostfildern-Ruit, 2000.

Rudick 2022
Rudick, Nicole. *What Is Now Known Was Once Only Imagined: An (Auto)biography of Niki de Saint Phalle*. New York, 2022.

Saint Phalle 1972
Saint Phalle, Niki de. *The Devouring Mothers (Story Book)*. London, 1972.

Saint Phalle 1999
Saint Phalle, Niki de. *Traces: An Autobiography, 1930–1949*. Lausanne, 1999.

Saint Phalle 2006
Saint Phalle, Niki de. *Harry and Me, 1950–1960: The Family Years*. Bern, 2006.

Schulz-Hoffmann 2008
Schulz-Hoffmann, Carla, ed. *Niki de Saint Phalle: My Art, My Dreams*. Munich, 2003.

Paris 1993
Niki de Saint Phalle: Tableaux éclatés. Edited by Pontus Hultén. Exh. cat. Musée d'Art Moderne de la Ville de Paris. Paris, 1993.

Paris 2014
Niki de Saint Phalle au Grand Palais. Exh. cat. Grand Palais, Paris, Issy-les-Moulineaux, 2014.

Paris and Bilbao 2015
Niki de Saint Phalle. Exh. cat. Grand Palais, Paris; Guggenheim Museum, Bilbao. Madrid, 2015.

Tokyo 2015
Niki de Saint Phalle. Exh. cat. The National Art Center, Tokyo. Tokyo, 2015.

Wimmer 2006
Wimmer, Dorothee. *Das Verschwinden des Ichs: Das Menschenbild in der französischen Kunst; Literatur und Philosophie um 1960*. Berlin, 2006.

Biography

Niki de Saint Phalle (1930–2002) is one of the most important artists and sculptors of her generation. Growing up in Paris and New York, she returned to Paris in the 1950s, where she began her artistic career with her legendary *Shooting Paintings* series, and her sensual female figures, the *Nanas*, made her popular beyond the art world.

Colophon

The concept of the A-Z series is based on an idea by Ulf Küster.

Author Katharina Sykora
Copyediting Aaron Bogart
Translation Steven Lindberg
Graphic design Torsten Köchlin, Joana Katte
Project management and picture editing
Juliane Eisele, Richard Viktor Hagemann
Typeface Scto Grotesk A
Production Kati Klaeske
Reproductions DLG, Paris
Paper Munken Lynx, 150 g/m²
Printing DZS GRAFIK, d. o. o., Ljubljana

Published by
Hatje Cantz Verlag GmbH
Mommsenstraße 27
10629 Berlin
Deutschland
www.hatjecantz.de

A Ganske Publishing Group Company

ISBN 978-3-7757-5437-8 (English edition)
ISBN 978-3-7757-5436-1 (German edition)

Printed in Slovenia

Cover illustrations
Nana Mosaïque Noire, 1999, photo: Pedrini, Photography, Zürich; *La Tempérance,* 1986/87, Galerie Hans Mayer; *Boule rouge Anne*, 1969, Museum Ulm, photo: Bernd Kegler, Ulm

Frontispiece
Niki de Saint Phalle with her work *Tea Party, ou Le Thé chez Angelina,* 1971, © Robert Doisneau/ GAMMA RAPHO; Visitors entering *Hon,* Moderna Museet, Stockholm, 1966, © Hans Hammarskiöld Heritage